T H E   B O O K   O F

AFTERNOON
Tea

THE   BOOK   OF

AFTERNOON
Tea

LESLEY MACKLEY

Photographed by
JON STEWART

HPBooks
a division of
PRICE STERN SLOAN
Los   Angeles

ANOTHER BEST SELLING VOLUME FROM HPBOOKS

HPBooks
A division of Price Stern Sloan, Inc.
11150 Olympic Boulevard
Suite 650
Los Angeles, California 90064
9 8 7 6 5 4 3 2 1

By arrangement with Salamander Books Ltd.

Home Economist: Sandra Baddeley
Printed in Belgium by Proost International Book Production

CONTENTS

INTRODUCTION 7

AFTERNOON TEA 8

SANDWICHES 10

SAVORIES 22

SCONES & MUFFINS 34

YEAST BREADS & QUICK BREADS 40

CAKES 50

SMALL CAKES 60

SPECIAL CAKES 70

PASTRIES 82

COOKIES 90

PRESERVES 102

DRINKS 106

SELECTIONS 112

INDEX 120

INTRODUCTION

As various food fads come and go, many people long to return to a more traditional and leisurely style of eating. And, in an age when everyone is constantly busy and short of time, what could be more enjoyable than taking time to indulge in what was once part of everyday life, but has now become a luxury—afternoon tea.

Afternoon tea is a perfect way of entertaining just a few friends, or a large crowd, and can be anything from an intimate gathering around a roaring fire on a winter's afternoon, to a relaxed party in the garden on a sunny summer's day.

With over 100 recipes (all with helpful step-by-step photographs), *The Book of Afternoon Tea* has recipes for every occasion. Some are old-fashioned favorites guaranteed to bring back nostalgic memories, and alongside are recipes our Victorian and Edwardian ancestors would certainly not recognize, but which are welcome additions to any tea table.

So, bring out your prettiest tablecloth and best china, and indulge your family and friends in a delightful treat.

——— AFTERNOON TEA ———

The custom of afternoon tea is thought to have been introduced in England in 1840 by Anna, the seventh Duchess of Bedford. Lunch was taken earlier then, and dinner was not served until about 9 o' clock. Not surprisingly, the Duchess became rather hungry during the afternoon and requested some tea, bread and butter and cake to be brought to her room. This quickly became a habit, and she started asking friends to join her.

It was soon fashionable to take tea in the middle of the afternoon, and the occasion became increasingly elaborate. Elegant tea accessories became available in the form of bone china tea services and delicate lace tablecloths, and the ladies would change into long tea gowns to preside over ornate silver teapots while engaging in lightweight conversation.

In Edwardian times, in Britain, tea shops flourished and, tea rooms in department stores became popular. Fashionable hotels serving elaborate and elegant afternoons teas were popular meeting places.

A TRADITIONAL AFTERNOON TEA

Afternoon tea has lost favor since World War II. Life is lived at a faster pace today, often making it impractical to stop in the middle of the afternoon for a leisurely cup of tea and cake. It is a habit well worth reviving, however, even if only for an occasional moment of self indulgence. Afternoon tea should be a graceful event; an opportunity to display the best china and table linen, and a time for people of all ages to gather together for relaxation and refreshments.

The choice of food served for afternoon tea depends on the occasion, the time of year and personal taste. A traditional tea consists of a selection of sandwiches and savories, followed by scones or cookies and preserves, pastries, cookies, plain cake and quick breads, with a more elaborate cake as a centerpiece. At a winter's fireside tea, toast and crumpets or muffins would be served with butter and savory or sweet spreads.

The essential drink to accompany afternoon tea is, of course, tea, but many other drinks are also traditionally served, depending on the time of year. In the summer, iced tea, fruit cordials and light fruit cups are very refreshing, and in the winter, spiced tea, or warming punches are always popular.

The type of tea to serve is a matter of personal taste, but it is a good idea to offer a choice of Indian or China tea, or a fragrant Earl Grey or Lapsang Souchong. Herbal or fruit teas are also becoming increasingly popular. China and other delicately flavored teas should be served with slices of lemon rather than milk.

MAKING TEA
It is worth taking trouble to produce a good cup of tea.
- Use the best quality tea you can afford.
- Fill the kettle with cold water.
- Warm the pot by rinsing with hot water.
- Use 1 teaspoon of tea for every 3/4 cup water.
- When the water is boiling, pour it onto the tea, replace the lid and steep 3 to 5 minutes.
- Serve tea freshly made.

─ CUCUMBER & DILL HEARTS ─

1/4 cucumber
1/2 teaspoon wine vinegar
1/2 teaspoon salt
3 tablespoons butter, softened
4 slices white bread
Pepper
1 teaspoon chopped fresh dill
TO GARNISH:
Dill sprigs

With a knife, peel cucumber, then cut into paper-thin slices. Place in a colander and sprinkle with vinegar and salt. Leave 30 minutes.

Pat cucumber slices dry on paper towels. Butter bread. Arrange cucumber slices on buttered sides of 2 bread slices. Season with pepper and scatter chopped dill over cucumber. Cover with remaining bread slices, buttered sides down, and press together.

Using a heart-shaped cookie cutter, cut out 4 heart shapes from each sandwich. Arrange on a serving plate and garnish with dill sprigs.

Makes 8.

——EGG & SPROUT CIRCLES——

4 eggs
4 tablespoons mayonnaise
1 teaspoon Dijon-style mustard
2 teaspoons Worcestershire sauce
Few drops hot-pepper sauce
Salt and pepper
6 tablespoons butter, softened
8 large slices white bread
Radish sprouts
TO GARNISH:
Radish sprouts

To a saucepan, add eggs and enough water to cover eggs. Bring to a boil, reduce heat and simmer about 12 minutes.

Drain eggs, crack shells lightly and place into a bowl of cold water until completely cold. Remove shells and coarsely chop eggs. Add mayonnaise, mustard, Worcestershire sauce, hot-pepper sauce, salt and pepper. Mix together well.

Butter bread. Spread egg mixture on buttered sides of 4 bread slices. Top with radish sprouts. Cover with remaining bread slices, buttered sides down, and press together. With a knife, cut off crusts from bread. Using a 2-inch round cookie cutter, cut out 4 circles from each sandwich. Arrange on a serving plate and garnish with radish sprouts.

Makes 16.

ITALIAN TEMPTERS

4 large slices white bread
3 tablespoons butter, softened
4 teaspoons pesto
4 small tomatoes
Salt and pepper
1/4 pound mozzarella cheese
TO GARNISH:
Fresh basil leaves

Spread slices of bread with butter. Using a 2-inch round cookie cutter, cut out 4 circles from each slice of bread.

Spread a little pesto over each buttered circle. With a knife, cut ends off each tomato, then cut each tomato into 4 slices. Place 1 slice on each bread circle. Season with salt and pepper to taste.

With knife, cut mozzarella into cubes. Arrange cubes on tomato slices. Arrange on a serving dish, garnished with fresh basil leaves.

Makes 16.

Note: Ready-made pesto is available in larger supermarkets, Italian delicatessens and specialty food stores.

——— STRIPED SANDWICHES ———

3 ounces sliced cooked ham
4 teaspoons mayonnaise
1/2 teaspoon Dijon-style mustard
1/4 cup cream cheese, softened
4 teaspoons chopped fresh chives
Salt and pepper
1/2 cup plus 1 tablespoon butter, softened
2 slices white bread
2 slices whole-wheat bread
TO GARNISH:
Fresh chives

With a knife, finely chop ham. Into a bowl, place ham, mayonnaise and mustard. Mix together well.

In another bowl, mix together cream cheese, chives, salt and pepper. Butter 2 slices each white and whole-wheat bread on one side only and the remaining 2 slices white and whole-wheat bread on both sides.

Spread half the ham mixture on buttered sides of 2 whole-wheat bread slices. Cover with white bread which has been buttered on both sides. Spread cream cheese mixture over white bread. Cover with brown bread which has been buttered on both sides, spread with remaining ham mixture and top with white bread, buttered side down. Remove crusts from bread. Cut each sandwich into 6 pieces. Arrange on a serving plate and garnish with chives.

Makes 12.

—— PASTRAMI SANDWICHES ——

1/2 cup watercress, large stems removed
4 ounces pastrami
1/4 cup cottage cheese
2 teaspoons mayonnaise
Salt and pepper
4 slices light rye bread
3 tablespoons butter, softened
TO GARNISH:
Watercress sprigs

With a knife, finely chop watercress. Finely chop pastrami.

In a bowl, mix together watercress, pastrami, cottage cheese, mayonnaise, salt and pepper.

Butter slices of bread. Spread pastrami mixture on buttered sides of 2 bread slices. Cover with remaining bread slices, buttered sides down, and press down. Cut off crusts from bread. Cut each sandwich into 4 triangles. Arrange on a serving plate and garnish with watercress.

Makes 8.

AVOCADO & BACON SANDWICHES

1/4 pound bacon slices
1 ripe avocado
1/2 teaspoon lemon juice
Salt and pepper
3 tablespoons butter, softened
4 large slices whole-wheat bread
TO GARNISH:
Lemon twist and parsley sprig

With a knife, coarsely chop bacon. Put into a skillet over medium heat and fry until bacon is crisp. Drain on paper towels.

Peel avocado, taking care not to remove bright green flesh just inside skin. Cut in half and remove seed. In a bowl, mash avocado, then stir in lemon juice, salt and pepper.

Butter bread. Spread avocado mixture on buttered sides of 2 bread slices. Scatter bacon over avocado. Cover with remaining bread slices, buttered sides down, and press together. With a knife, cut off crusts. Cut each sandwich into 4 triangles. Arrange on a serving plate, garnished with a lemon twist and parsley sprig.

Makes 8.

— SPICY CHICKEN SANDWICHES —

1/4 pound boneless cooked chicken
2 teaspoons mango chutney
2-1/2 tablespoons mayonnaise
1/2 teaspoon curry powder
1 teaspoon lime juice
Salt
3 tablespoons butter, softened
4 slices whole-wheat bread
TO GARNISH:
Lime twist and dill sprig

With a sharp knife, chop chicken into small pieces, then set aside.

With a sharp knife, chop up any large pieces of fruit in the chutney. In a bowl, combine chutney with mayonnaise, curry powder, lime juice and salt. Mix together well. Stir in chopped chicken.

Butter bread. Divide chicken mixture between buttered sides of 2 bread slices. Cover with remaining bread slices, buttered side down, and press together. Cut off crusts from bread. Cut each sandwich into 4 rectangles. Arrange on a serving plate, garnished with a lime twist and a dill sprig.

Makes 8.

TURKEY TRIANGLES

3 tablespoons butter, softened
4 slices white bread
4 crisp lettuce leaves
3 ounces boneless cooked turkey, thinly sliced
Salt and pepper
4 teaspoons cranberry sauce
TO GARNISH:
Small pickles, cut into fan shapes

Butter bread. Arrange lettuce leaves over buttered sides of 2 bread slices.

Arrange sliced turkey over lettuce. Season with salt and pepper to taste. Spread cranberry sauce over remaining bread slices, then place cranberry side down over turkey. Press together.

With a sharp knife, cut off crusts from bread. Cut each sandwich into 4 triangles. Arrange on a serving plate, garnished with pickles.

Makes 8.

Variation: Cranberry jelly may be used instead of cranberry sauce, if desired.

SHRIMP FINGERS

1/2 cup whipping cream
1 teaspoon tomato paste
1 teaspoon lemon juice
Few drops hot-pepper sauce
Salt
1/4 pound shelled cooked shrimp, thawed if frozen
4 small oval rolls
1/4 cup butter, softened
Red (cayenne) pepper
TO GARNISH:
Cucumber slices, shrimp and mint sprigs

In a bowl, whip cream until thick enough to hold soft peaks.

Add tomato paste, lemon juice, hot-pepper sauce and salt. Mix together gently. Pat shrimp dry with paper towels and add to cream mixture.

Cut rolls in half lengthwise and butter each half. Spread shrimp mixture on bottom half of each buttered roll. Arrange on a serving plate. Sprinkle with cayenne and replace top. Garnish with cucumber slices, shrimp and mint sprigs.

Makes 4.

SALMON PINWHEELS

1 large unsliced sandwich loaf
1/4 cup butter, softened
2 ounces watercress
1/4 pound thinly sliced smoked salmon
Pepper
1 teaspoon lemon juice
TO GARNISH:
Watercress

With a sharp knife, cut crusts from loaf of bread. Cut 2 (2-inch-thick) lengthwise slices from loaf. Using a rolling pin, roll each slice of bread firmly to flatten.

Spread butter over slices of bread. Remove stems from watercress and arrange leaves over buttered sides of slices. Arrange slices of smoked salmon over the watercress. Season with pepper and sprinkle with lemon juice.

Roll up each slice, like a jellyroll, starting from a short side. Wrap rolls tightly in plastic wrap and refrigerate at least 2 hours. Remove plastic wrap and cut each roll into 7 pinwheels. Arrange on a serving plate, garnished with watercress.

Makes 14.

──STILTON & PEAR POCKETS──

4 pita breads
2 ripe pears
2 ounces Stilton cheese, crumbled
1/2 cup chopped walnuts
TO GARNISH:
Lettuce leaves

Preheat broiler. Broil pita breads lightly so they puff up. Cut each pita bread in half through center. Open each half to make a pocket.

Peel pears, remove cores and chop flesh coarsely. In a bowl, combine pears with crumbled Stilton cheese and chopped walnuts and mix together.

Divide pear mixture among pita pockets. Arrange on a serving plate, garnished with lettuce leaves. Serve at once.

Makes 8.

DATE & WALNUT SANDWICHES

1/2 cup dates
1/3 cup walnuts
3 tablespoons cream cheese, softened
4 large slices or 8 small slices fruit bread
1 tablespoon honey
Pinch of ground cinnamon
TO DECORATE:
A few dates and walnuts

With a sharp knife, finely chop dates. Finely chop walnuts.

Spread cream cheese onto all the bread slices. Spread honey over half the slices on top of the cheese. Scatter dates and walnuts over the honey-coated slices and sprinkle with cinnamon.

Cover with remaining bread slices, cheese sides down, and press together. With a knife, cut off crusts from bread. Cut large sandwiches into 4 squares or small ones in half. Arrange on a serving plate, decorated with dates and walnuts.

Makes 8.

Variation: White or whole-wheat bread may be used instead of fruit bread.

SALAMI PUFFS

6 ounces puff pastry dough, thawed if frozen
8 slices Italian salami
1/4 cup shredded Cheddar cheese (1 ounce)
1 egg, to glaze
TO GARNISH:
Mâche leaves or parsley sprigs

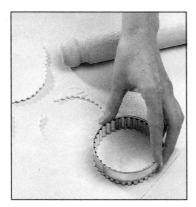

Preheat oven to 400F (205C). On a floured surface, roll out puff pastry dough to 1/8 inch thick. Using a 4-inch fluted cookie cutter, cut out 8 circles of dough.

Lay a slice of salami in center of each dough circle. Put a little cheese on each salami slice.

In a bowl, beat egg, then brush egg around edges of dough. Fold dough circle in half and press edges firmly to seal. Brush top of each puff with beaten egg. Bake 15 minutes, until well risen and golden-brown. Serve garnished with mâche leaves or parsley.

Makes 8.

——— DEVILED HAM TOASTS ———

1/4 pound lean cooked ham
1 tablespoon Worcestershire sauce
Red (cayenne) pepper, to taste
2 teaspoons Dijon-style mustard
6 slices bread
1/4 cup butter, softened
TO GARNISH:
3 pimento-stuffed olives, sliced
Watercress sprigs

With a sharp knife, chop ham very finely, or mince. In a bowl, mix together ham, Worcestershire sauce, cayenne and mustard.

Toast bread. Using a 2-inch plain, round cookie cutter, cut out 2 circles from each slice of toast. Butter each circle of toast using 2 tablespoons of the butter and keep warm. In a saucepan, melt remaining butter. Add ham mixture. Cook, stirring, over low heat until mixture is hot.

Spread ham mixture over toast circles. Garnish with olives and arrange on a serving plate with watercress sprigs. Serve at once.

Makes 12 servings.

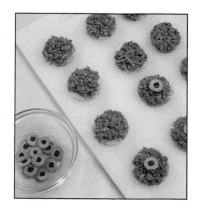

POTTED SHRIMP

3/4 pound shelled cooked small shrimp
Salt
Red (cayenne) pepper, to taste
1 teaspoon lemon juice
1/2 teaspoon ground ginger
3/4 cup butter
1 tablespoon finely chopped fresh chives
TO GARNISH:
Chives
TO SERVE:
French bread or buttered toast

If using thawed, frozen shrimp, pat dry with paper towels.

In a bowl, combine shrimp, salt, cayenne, lemon juice and ginger. Cover and refrigerate. In a saucepan, melt butter over very low heat. Pour the clear liquid into a bowl, leaving the milky residue in pan to be discarded. Stir chopped chives into clear liquid. Let stand 20 minutes.

Divide shrimp among 6 small ramekin dishes. Spoon chive butter over, pressing shrimp down until covered with butter. Cover and refrigerate until firm. Garnish with chives, and serve with French bread or toast.

Makes 6 servings.

—CRAB & GINGER TRIANGLES—

1 (7-oz.) can crabmeat, drained
6 green onions, finely chopped
1-inch piece gingerroot, peeled and grated
2 teaspoons soy sauce
Salt and pepper
6 large sheets filo pastry, each about 14 inches square
6 tablespoons butter, melted
TO GARNISH:
Green onion slivers or curls

In a bowl, mix together crabmeat, green onions, gingerroot, soy sauce, salt and pepper. Set aside.

Preheat oven to 350F (175C). Lightly grease a baking sheet. Work with 1 sheet of pastry at a time, keeping remainder covered with a damp cloth. Cut sheet of pastry in half. Brush each half with melted butter and fold in half lengthwise. Brush pastry all over with melted butter. Put a portion of crab mixture in 1 corner of 1 strip of pastry. Fold pastry and filling over at right angles to make a triangle, then continue folding in this way along strip of pastry to make a triangular package.

Repeat with remaining pastry and crab mixture. Brush each triangle with melted butter. Bake 20 to 25 minutes, until crisp and golden-brown. Serve warm, garnished with green onion slivers or curls.

Makes 12.

———— TUNA TOASTIES ————

1 (7-oz.) can tuna
3 tomatoes
3 ounces Cheddar cheese
4 slices bread
2 tablespoons butter, softened
TO GARNISH:
Dill sprigs

Preheat oven to 400F (205C). Drain tuna. Into a bowl, place tuna and flake. With a knife, slice tomatoes. Shred cheese.

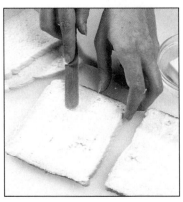

Spread one side of each slice of bread with butter. Place buttered sides down on a baking sheet.

Spread tuna over bread. Arrange tomatoes on top and cover with shredded cheese. Bake 8 to 10 minutes, until bubbling. Cool 1 minute, then cut each slice of bread across into 2 triangles. Serve hot, garnished with dill.

Makes 8.

— SMOKED SALMON CROÛTES —

2/3 cup dairy sour cream
1/4 cup butter
1 tablespoon vegetable oil
8 (2-inch-thick) round bread slices
1/4 pound smoked salmon
TO GARNISH:
Dill sprigs

In a bowl, beat sour cream until thick and smooth. Set aside. In a skillet, heat butter and oil. Add bread and cook on both sides until golden. Drain on paper towels and keep warm.

Cut smoked salmon into about 5″ × 3/4″ strips and roll each one up loosely.

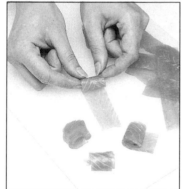

Place 4 rolls of smoked salmon on each croûte. Spoon a little of the sour cream over salmon. Garnish each croûte with a dill sprig.

Makes 8.

PARMESAN BEIGNETS

1/4 cup butter
1/2 cup plus 2 tablespoons all-purpose flour, sifted
2 eggs, beaten
1 teaspoon chopped fresh parsley
1/2 cup grated Parmesan cheese (1-1/2 ounces)
1/4 cup shredded Cheddar cheese (1 ounce)
Salt and pepper
Vegetable oil for deep-frying
TO GARNISH:
Parsley sprigs

In a large pan, melt butter. Add 2/3 cup water and bring to a boil.

Add flour, all at once, and beat thoroughly until mixture leaves the side of the pan. Cool slightly, then vigorously beat in eggs, a little at a time. Stir in parsley, cheeses, salt and pepper. Continue beating until cheeses have melted.

One-third fill a deep-fat fryer with vegetable oil and heat to 360F (180C). Carefully drop 4 or 5 walnut-size spoonfuls of dough into hot oil. Deep-fry 2 to 3 minutes, until puffed and golden-brown. Drain well on paper towels and keep warm until all the beignets are fried. Serve garnished with parsley sprigs.

Makes about 16.

——WELSH RABBIT FINGERS——

1/2 pound sharp Cheddar cheese
2 tablespoons butter, softened
1 tablespoon Worcestershire sauce
1 teaspoon mustard powder
1 tablespoon all-purpose flour
About 1/4 cup beer
4 slices whole-wheat bread
TO GARNISH:
Red (cayenne) pepper for dusting
Red bell pepper strips
Parsley sprigs

Preheat broiler. Into a bowl, shred cheese. Add butter, Worcestershire sauce, mustard, flour and enough beer to make a stiff paste.

Toast bread on both sides. Spread cheese mixture over one side of each slice of toast.

Broil until topping is cooked through and well browned. Dust with cayenne. Cut each slice of toast into 3 rectangles. Garnish with bell pepper strips and parsley sprigs.

Makes 12.

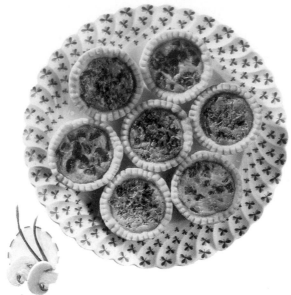

MINI QUICHES

1-1/2 recipes Pie Crust Dough (page 89)
3 egg yolks
1 egg
Salt and pepper
1-1/4 cups whipping cream
MUSHROOM FILLING:
1 tablespoon butter
1-1/2 cups finely chopped mushrooms
BELL PEPPER FILLING:
1 tablespoon butter
1 red bell pepper, chopped

Preheat oven to 400F (205C). Grease 12 individual 2-1/2-inch quiche pans.

To make mushroom filling, in a small pan, melt the 1 tablespoon butter. Add mushrooms and cook gently until softened and all liquid has evaporated. Set aside. To make bell pepper filling, in another small pan, melt remaining 1 tablespoon butter. Add bell pepper and cook gently until beginning to soften. Set aside. On a floured surface, roll out pastry to 1/8 inch thick. Use to line prepared pans; prick bottoms with a fork.

Press a square of foil into each dough case. Bake blind 15 minutes, removing foil after 12 minutes. In a bowl, beat together egg yolks, egg, salt, pepper and cream. Put half the mixture in a bowl with the mushrooms and half in a bowl with the bell pepper. Divide the 2 fillings among baked pastry shells. Return to oven and cook 15 minutes longer, just until firm. Serve warm or at room temperature.

Makes 12.

POTTED STILTON

1/2 pound Stilton cheese
1/4 cup unsalted butter, softened
2 tablespoons brandy
1/2 cup chopped walnuts
Pinch of red (cayenne) pepper
TO FINISH:
2 tablespoons butter
TO GARNISH:
Walnut halves

Into a bowl, crumble Stilton. Add the 1/4 cup butter and work into Stilton with a wooden spoon until well blended.

Mix in brandy, chopped walnuts and cayenne. Pack mixture into 4 ramekin dishes.

In a small saucepan, melt remaining butter over very low heat. Pour clear liquid over cheese mixture, leaving milky residue in the pan to be discarded. Leave potted Stilton to cool. Serve garnished with walnut halves. Serve with crackers.

Makes 4 servings.

Variation: Instead of Stilton, use finely shredded Cheddar cheese. Port may be used instead of brandy, if desired.

CHEESE STRAWS

1 cup all-purpose flour
Pinch of salt
1/2 teaspoon curry powder
1/4 cup butter, chilled
1/2 cup shredded Cheddar cheese (2 ounces)
1 egg, beaten
TO FINISH:
Poppy seeds and cumin seeds

Into a bowl, sift flour, salt and curry powder. Cut in butter until mixture resembles fine bread crumbs. Add cheese and half of the egg and mix to form a dough. Cover and refrigerate at least 30 minutes.

Preheat oven to 400F (205C). Butter several baking sheets. On a floured surface, roll out dough to 1/4 inch thick. Cut into 3" × 1/2" strips. Twist and place on baking sheets.

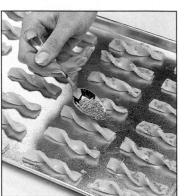

Brush cheese straws with remaining egg. Sprinkle half with poppy seeds and half with cumin seeds. Bake 10 to 15 minutes, until golden.

Makes 24 to 30.

SCOTCH EGGS

1/2 pound pork sausage
1 tablespoon chopped fresh chives
Salt and pepper
8 hard-boiled quails' eggs
All-purpose flour for coating
1 egg, beaten
1-1/2 cups fresh white bread crumbs
Vegetable oil for deep-frying

Into a bowl, put sausage. Mix in chives, salt and pepper. Divide into 8 equal portions. On a floured surface, flatten each piece into a 2-inch circle.

Shell eggs and dust with flour. Put beaten egg in one dish and bread crumbs in another. Place each egg on a circle of sausage. Mold sausage around egg, sealing seams well.

Roll each sausage-covered egg in beaten egg, then in bread crumbs. One-third fill a deep-fat fryer with vegetable oil and heat to 360F (180C). Carefully put eggs into oil and deep-fry 3 to 4 minutes, until golden-brown. Drain well on paper towels until cool.

Makes 8.

Variation: Instead of quails' eggs, use 4 chicken eggs and cook 5 to 6 minutes.

SCONES

2 cups self-rising flour, plus extra for dusting
1 teaspoon baking powder
1/4 cup butter, chilled
5 teaspoons sugar
2/3 cup milk
TO SERVE:
Butter or whipped cream and jam

Preheat oven to 425F (220C). Dust a baking sheet with flour. Into a bowl, sift flour and baking powder, then stir to mix. Cut in butter, then stir in sugar.

Make a well in the center of the mixture and pour in milk. Using a knife, mix together until dough is soft, but not sticky. Turn out dough onto a floured surface and knead lightly. Pat dough out to 1/2 inch thick.

Using a 2-inch round cookie cutter, cut out 12 scones. Arrange on prepared baking sheet and dust the tops with flour. Bake 10 to 12 minutes, until well risen and light brown. Transfer to a wire rack and cover with a cloth while cooling. Serve with butter or whipped cream and jam.

Makes 12.

Variation: For Cheese Scones, omit sugar and stir in 1/2 cup shredded Cheddar cheese.

SCOTCH PANCAKES

2 cups self-rising flour
2 teaspoons baking powder
Pinch of salt
5 teaspoons sugar
1 egg, beaten
1 cup milk
ORANGE BUTTER:
3/4 cup unsalted butter, softened
2 tablespoons powdered sugar, sifted
2 tablespoons fresh orange juice
Shredded zest of 1/2 orange

To make Orange Butter, in a bowl, beat together all ingredients until light and fluffy. To make pancakes, into another bowl, sift flour, baking powder and salt. Stir in sugar and make a well in center. In another bowl, mix together egg and milk, then pour into well. Gradually draw flour into liquid by stirring with a wooden spoon, then beat well to make a smooth batter.

Slowly heat a greased griddle or heavy-bottomed skillet. Drop spoonfuls of batter onto hot pan and cook about 3 minutes, until bubbles burst on surface and underside is golden. Turn pancakes over with a spatula and cook 1 minute longer, until golden on second side. Wrap in a cloth to keep warm until all pancakes are cooked. Serve with Orange Butter.

Makes 20 to 24.

——— APPLE BISCUIT ROUND ———

2 cups all-purpose flour
2 teaspoons baking powder
1/2 cup butter, chilled
2 apples
1/2 cup sugar
1/3 cup golden raisins
1 egg, beaten
TO FINISH:
1 tablespoon granulated brown sugar
TO SERVE:
Butter

Preheat oven to 350F (175C). Grease an 8-inch round cake pan. Into a bowl, sift flour and baking powder.

Cut in butter until mixture resembles bread crumbs. Peel and core apples, cut into small dice and stir into flour and butter mixture with sugar and golden raisins. Stir in beaten egg to form a soft dough. Press mixture into prepared pan. Sprinkle brown sugar on top.

Bake 40 to 50 minutes, until risen and golden-brown. Turn out onto a wire rack and leave until just warm. Cut biscuit in half horizontally. Spread bottom with butter and replace top. Cut into wedges and serve.

Makes 8 wedges.

BLACKBERRY MUFFINS

2-1/2 cups all-purpose flour
1 tablespoon baking powder
1/2 cup sugar
1 egg
1-1/3 cups milk
6 tablespoons vegetable oil
1 teaspoon vanilla extract
6 ounces blackberries
TO FINISH:
2 tablespoons granulated brown sugar

Preheat oven to 400F (205C). Grease a 12-cup muffin pan. Into a bowl, sift flour and baking powder. Stir in sugar.

In another bowl, beat together egg, milk, oil and vanilla. Add to dry ingredients all at once. Stir just until blended. Gently stir in blackberries.

Spoon batter into prepared muffin pan. Sprinkle with brown sugar. Bake 15 to 20 minutes, until well risen and golden-brown. Cool in pan 5 minutes, then turn out muffins onto a wire rack to cool completely.

Makes 12.

WELSH CAKES

2 cups self-rising flour
Pinch of salt
1/4 cup vegetable shortening
1/4 cup margarine, chilled
2/3 cup sugar
2/3 cup dried currants
1 egg, beaten
1 tablespoon milk (optional)
TO FINISH:
Sugar for dusting

Into a bowl, sift flour and salt. Cut in shortening and margarine until mixture resembles bread crumbs. Stir in sugar and currants.

Add egg and a little milk, if necessary, to make a soft, but not sticky dough. On a floured surface, roll out dough to 1/4 inch thick. Using a 2-1/2-inch plain or fluted round cookie cutter, cut out about 16 circles.

Heat a greased griddle or heavy-bottomed skillet. Cook cakes, over low heat, about 3 minutes on each side until golden-brown. Dust with sugar.

Makes about 16.

— CHOCOLATE-NUT MUFFINS —

4 ounces semisweet chocolate
2 cups all-purpose flour
1 tablespoon baking powder
1/2 teaspoon ground cinnamon
1/3 cup packed brown sugar
1 cup coarsely chopped walnuts
1 cup milk
1/4 cup vegetable oil
1 teaspoon vanilla extract
1 egg

Preheat oven to 400F (205C). Grease a 12-cup muffin pan.

Into a heatproof bowl set over a pan of simmering water, break chocolate and heat until melted. Remove from heat.

Into bowl of chocolate, sift flour, baking powder and cinnamon. Add sugar and nuts. In another bowl, mix together milk, oil, vanilla and egg. Add to dry ingredients and stir just until blended. Spoon batter into prepared pan. Bake 15 to 20 minutes, until well risen and firm to the touch. Cool in pan 5 minutes, then turn out muffins onto a wire rack to cool completely.

Makes 12.

——DATE & WALNUT LOAF——

1/2 pound pitted dates
Grated zest and juice of 1 lemon
1/3 cup water
3/4 cup butter, softened
1 cup packed light brown sugar
3 eggs, beaten
1-1/2 cups self-rising flour
1/2 cup chopped walnuts
TO FINISH:
8 walnut halves

Preheat oven to 325F (165C). Grease and line the bottom of a 9″ × 5″ loaf pan with waxed paper. Chop dates.

Into a saucepan, put dates with lemon zest and juice and water. Cook 5 minutes, until a soft puree. In a bowl, beat butter and sugar together until light and fluffy. Gradually beat in eggs. Fold in flour and chopped walnuts. Spread one-third of batter over bottom of prepared pan. Spread half the date puree over batter. Repeat layers, ending with cake batter.

Arrange halved walnuts in a line down center of loaf. Bake 1 to 1-1/2 hours, until well risen and firm to the touch. Cool loaf in pan 10 minutes, then turn out loaf, peel off lining paper and transfer to a wire rack to cool completely. Serve sliced.

Makes 10 to 12 slices.

CHERRY-NUT BREAD

3 cups bread flour
1/2 teaspoon salt
1 teaspoon sugar
2 teaspoons active dry yeast
1/4 cup butter, chilled
1/3 cup candied cherries, chopped
1/2 cup chopped walnuts
2/3 cup lukewarm milk (130F, 55C)
1/3 cup lukewarm water (130F, 55C)
1 egg, beaten
TOPPING:
1/2 cup powdered sugar, sifted
2 tablespoons candied cherries
1/3 cup walnut halves

Grease and flour a baking sheet. Into a bowl, sift flour. Stir in salt, sugar and yeast. Cut in butter, and add chopped cherries and walnuts. Make a well in center. Pour in milk, water and egg. Mix to a soft dough. Turn dough out onto a floured surface and knead 10 minutes, until smooth. Put in an oiled bowl, cover and leave in a warm place until doubled in bulk. Turn dough out onto a floured surface, knead lightly and divide into 5 pieces. Roll each out to a rope 12 inches long.

Braid 3 ropes together and place on prepared baking sheet. Twist the remaining 2 ropes together and place on top. Cover with oiled plastic wrap. Leave in a warm place until doubled in bulk. Preheat oven to 425F (220C). Bake 10 minutes, then reduce heat to 375F (190C) and bake 20 minutes longer. Cool. Mix powdered sugar with enough water to make a thin frosting; drizzle over loaf. Decorate with cherries and walnuts.

Makes about 12 slices.

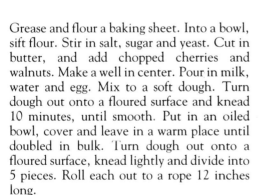

——CARAWAY KUGELHOPF——

2 cups all-purpose flour
1/4 cup sugar
2 teaspoons active dry yeast
2 tablespoons caraway seeds
1/4 cup lukewarm water (130F, 55C)
1/2 cup unsalted butter, melted
3 eggs, beaten
TO FINISH:
Powdered sugar

Grease an 8-inch kugelhopf mold. Into a bowl, sift flour. Stir in sugar, yeast and caraway seeds.

Make a well in center. Stir in water, butter and eggs. Beat vigorously until smooth. Cover bowl with plastic wrap and leave in a warm place until doubled in bulk. Stir mixture and pour into prepared mold. Cover with plastic wrap and leave to rise again until doubled in bulk.

Preheat oven to 400F (205C). Bake kugelhopf 20 minutes. Reduce temperature to 375F (190C) and bake 10 minutes longer, until well risen and golden-brown. Cool in the mold 10 minutes, then turn out kugelhopf and transfer to a wire rack. Dust lightly with powdered sugar. Serve with butter while still slightly warm.

Makes 8 to 10 slices.

Note: Eggs should be at room temperature.

── CRANBERRY-BRAZIL LOAF ──

2 cups all-purpose flour
1 tablespoon baking powder
1 teaspoon ground cinnamon
1/2 cup sugar
2 eggs
Grated zest of 1 orange
1/2 cup orange juice
1/2 cup chopped Brazil nuts
3/4 cup cranberries
1/4 cup plus 1 tablespoon butter, melted

Preheat oven to 350F (175C). Grease and line a 9″ × 5″ loaf pan with waxed paper.

Into a bowl, sift flour, baking powder and cinnamon. Stir in sugar and make a well in center. In another bowl, beat eggs with orange zest and juice. Pour into dry ingredients and stir just until combined.

Stir in Brazil nuts, cranberries and melted butter. Pour into prepared pan. Bake 50 minutes, until well risen and browned. Turn out loaf, peel off lining paper, then transfer to a wire rack to cool completely. When cool, wrap in foil and keep 24 hours before serving, sliced, with butter.

Makes 10 to 12 slices.

——LEEK & BACON KNOTS——

1 leek, finely chopped
1/4 cup butter, chilled
6 ounces bacon slices, chopped
2 cups bread flour
2 cups whole-wheat flour
1 teaspoon salt
1 teaspoon sugar
2 teaspoons active dry yeast
2/3 cup lukewarm milk (130F, 55C)
3/4 cup lukewarm water (130F, 55C)
TO FINISH:
1 egg, beaten, and sesame seeds

Into a skillet, put leek and half the butter.
Cook over low heat until leek is softened.

Remove leek from pan and cool. In same
skillet, cook bacon until slightly crisp. Let
cool. Into a bowl, sift bread flour. Stir in
whole-wheat flour, salt, sugar and yeast. Cut
in remaining butter. Stir in leek and bacon.
Make a well in center. Pour in milk and
water. Stir until a soft dough is formed. Turn
dough out onto a floured surface and knead
about 10 minutes, until smooth. Put in an
oiled bowl, cover and leave in a warm place
until doubled in bulk.

Grease 2 baking sheets. Turn dough onto a
floured surface and knead 3 to 4 minutes,
until smooth. Divide into 12 pieces, then roll
each into a rope about 12 inches long. Tie
each one in a knot and place on baking
sheets. Cover with plastic wrap and leave in a
warm place until doubled in size. Preheat
oven to 425F (220C). Brush rolls with egg
and sprinkle with sesame seeds. Bake 15
minutes, until golden. Cool on a wire rack.

Makes 12.

——— CHEESE & CHIVE BRAID ———

4 cups bread flour
1 teaspoon salt
1 teaspoon sugar
1-1/2 teaspoons active dry yeast
2 tablespoons butter, chilled
1 cup shredded Cheddar cheese (4 ounces)
3 tablespoons snipped fresh chives
4 green onions, chopped
2/3 cup lukewarm milk (130F, 55C)
3/4 cup lukewarm water (130F, 55C)
Beaten egg, to glaze

Into a bowl, sift flour. Stir in salt, sugar and yeast. Cut in butter.

Stir in cheese, chives and green onions and make a well in the center. Mix milk with water, then pour into the well. Mix until a soft dough is formed. Turn out dough onto a lightly floured surface. Knead about 10 minutes, until smooth and elastic. Place in an oiled bowl, cover and leave in a warm place about 1 hour, until doubled in bulk. Turn dough out onto a floured surface and knead about 3 minutes.

Divide dough into 3 pieces. Roll each one out to a long rope and braid together, pinching ends to seal. Place on a baking sheet, cover with oiled plastic wrap and leave in a warm place about 45 minutes, until doubled in bulk. Preheat oven to 425F (220C). Brush with beaten egg and bake 20 minutes. Reduce temperature to 350F (175C) and bake 15 minutes longer, until golden-brown and the bottom sounds hollow when tapped. Serve warm or cold with cheese and a salad.

Makes about 10 slices.

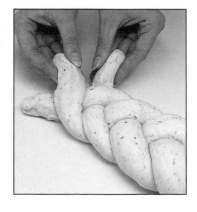

CHELSEA BUNS

2 cups bread flour
2 teaspoons active dry yeast
1 teaspoon sugar
1/2 teaspoon salt
2 tablespoons unsalted butter, chilled
1/2 cup lukewarm milk (130F, 55C)
1 egg, beaten
FILLING:
1/4 cup unsalted butter, softened
1/3 cup packed light brown sugar
3/4 cup chopped mixed dried fruit
1 teaspoon apple pie spice
TO FINISH:
1/2 cup powdered sugar

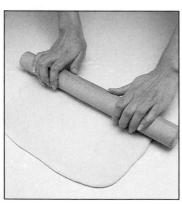

Butter an 8-inch square cake pan. Into a bowl, sift flour. Stir in yeast, sugar and salt. Cut in butter. Make a well in center. Pour in milk and egg and beat vigorously to make a soft dough. On a floured surface, knead dough 5 to 10 minutes, until smooth. Put dough in an oiled bowl, cover and leave in a warm place about 1 hour, until doubled in bulk. Turn dough out onto a floured surface. Knead lightly. Roll out to a 12" × 9" rectangle.

Spread with butter, then sprinkle with brown sugar, fruit and spice. Roll up from a long side and cut into 9 pieces. Place in pan, cut sides up. Cover with oiled plastic wrap. Leave in a warm place 45 minutes, until almost doubled in bulk. Preheat oven to 375F (190C). Bake 30 minutes, until golden. Cool in pan 10 minutes, then turn out and transfer in one piece to a wire rack to cool. Mix powdered sugar with enough water to make a thin glaze. Brush over buns. Leave to cool.

Makes 9.

LEMON & CURRANT BRIOCHES

2 cups bread flour
2 teaspoons active dry yeast
1/2 teaspoon salt
1 tablespoon sugar
1/3 cup dried currants
Grated zest of 1 lemon
2 tablespoons lukewarm water (130F, 55C)
2 eggs, beaten
1/4 cup unsalted butter, melted
TO GLAZE:
1 egg, beaten

Butter 12 individual brioche molds. Into a bowl, sift flour. Stir in yeast, salt, sugar, currants and lemon zest.

Make a well in center. Pour in water, eggs and melted butter and beat vigorously to make a soft dough. Turn dough out onto a lightly floured surface and knead 5 minutes, until smooth and elastic. Put dough in an oiled bowl, cover and leave in a warm place 1 hour, until doubled in bulk. Turn dough out onto a lightly floured surface, reknead and roll into a rope shape. Cut into 12 equal pieces. Shape three quarters of each piece into a ball and place in prepared molds.

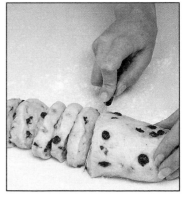

With a floured finger, press a hole in center of each. Shape remaining dough into little plugs, then press into holes, flattening the tops slightly. Place molds on a baking sheet. Cover with oiled plastic wrap and leave in a warm place until dough comes almost to top of molds. Preheat oven to 425F (220C). Brush brioches with beaten egg. Bake 15 minutes, until golden-brown. Serve warm.

Makes 12.

Note: Eggs should be at room temperature.

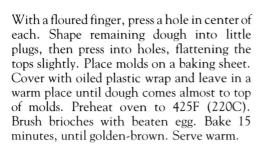

CRUMPETS

4 cups bread flour
1 teaspoon salt
1 teaspoon sugar
2 teaspoons active dry yeast
2-1/2 cups lukewarm milk (130F, 55C)
2/3 cup lukewarm water (130F, 55C)
Vegetable oil for cooking
TO SERVE:
Butter and jam

Into a bowl, sift flour. Stir in salt, sugar and yeast.

Make a well in center of flour and pour in milk and water. With a wooden spoon, gradually work flour into liquid, then beat vigorously to make a smooth batter. Cover bowl with a cloth and leave in a warm place 1 hour or until batter has doubled in bulk.

Thoroughly grease a heavy skillet or griddle and several crumpet rings or round cookie cutters. Arrange as many rings as possible in pan. Heat pan, then pour in enough batter to half fill each ring. Cook crumpets 5 to 6 minutes, until bubbles appear and burst on the surface. Remove rings and turn crumpets over. Cook on other side 2 to 3 minutes longer. Return rings to skillet to heat and repeat with remaining batter. Serve crumpets hot, generously buttered, with jam.

Makes about 16.

DEVONSHIRE SPLITS

1/4 cup unsalted butter
2 tablespoons sugar
2/3 cup milk
2/3 cup water
4 cups bread flour
2 teaspoons active dry yeast
1/2 teaspoon salt
FILLING:
1/3 cup strawberry jam
1-1/4 cups whipping cream, whipped
TO FINISH:
Powdered sugar for dusting

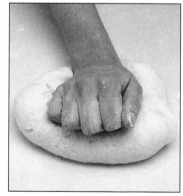

In a saucepan, heat butter, sugar, milk and water until sugar has dissolved.

Let mixture stand until lukewarm (130F, 55C). Into a bowl, sift flour. Stir in yeast and salt. Make a well in center, then pour in liquid and mix vigorously to make a soft dough. On a lightly floured surface, turn out dough and knead until smooth. Place in an oiled bowl, cover and leave in a warm place until doubled in bulk. Grease 2 baking sheets.

Turn dough out onto a floured surface. Divide into 16 pieces. Knead each piece lightly and shape into a ball. Place on baking sheets, flattening each ball slightly. Cover with oiled plastic wrap and leave in a warm place about 40 minutes, until well risen. Preheat oven to 425F (220C). Bake about 15 minutes, until bottoms sound hollow when tapped. Cool on a wire rack. Split and fill with jam and cream. Dust lightly with powdered sugar.

Makes 16.

——— LEMON CRUNCH CAKE ———

1/2 cup butter or margarine, softened
3/4 cup sugar
2 eggs, beaten
Finely grated zest of 1 lemon
1-1/2 cups self-rising flour, sifted
1/4 cup milk
TOPPING:
Juice of 1 lemon
1/2 cup sugar

Preheat oven to 350F (175C). Grease a 9" × 7" or an 8-inch square baking pan and line with waxed paper. In a bowl, beat together butter and sugar until light and fluffy.

Gradually beat in eggs. Stir in lemon zest. Fold in sifted flour, alternately with milk. Pour batter into prepared pan and level surface with a metal spatula. Bake about 50 minutes, until well risen and pale golden.

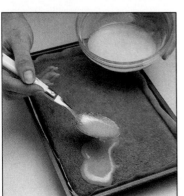

While cake is baking, make topping. In a bowl, mix together lemon juice and sugar. Spoon topping over hot cake. Leave cake in pan until completely cold, then turn out cake and cut into squares or diamonds.

Makes 12 squares or diamonds.

GINGER CAKE

2 cups self-rising flour
1 tablespoon ground ginger
1 teaspoon ground cinnamon
1/2 teaspoon baking soda
1/2 cup butter or margarine, chilled
3/4 cup packed light brown sugar
2 eggs
5 teaspoons light corn syrup
5 teaspoons milk
TOPPING:
3 pieces stem ginger
3/4 cup powdered sugar
4 teaspoons stem ginger syrup

Preheat oven to 325F (165C). Grease an 11″
× 7″ baking pan and line with waxed paper.
Into a bowl, sift flour, ginger, cinnamon and
baking soda. Cut in butter, then stir in sugar.
In another bowl, beat together eggs, syrup
and milk. Pour into dry ingredients and beat
until smooth and glossy. Pour batter into
pan. Bake 45 to 50 minutes, until well risen
and firm to the touch. Cool in pan 30
minutes, then transfer to a wire rack to cool
completely.

Cut each piece of stem ginger into quarters
and arrange on top of cake. In a bowl, mix
together powdered sugar, ginger syrup and
enough water to make a smooth frosting. Put
frosting into a waxed-paper pastry bag and
drizzle frosting over top of cake. Let set. Cut
cake into squares.

Makes 12 pieces.

JEWEL-TOPPED MADEIRA CAKE

1 cup butter, softened
1-1/4 cups sugar
Grated zest of 1 lemon
4 eggs, beaten
2 cups self-rising flour, sifted
3 tablespoons milk
TOPPING:
2-2/3 tablespoons honey
1/2 pound glacéd fruits and angelica

Preheat oven to 325F (165C). Grease and line an 8-inch springform cake pan with waxed paper. In a bowl, beat together butter, sugar and lemon zest until light and fluffy. Gradually beat in eggs. Fold in flour, alternately with milk. Spoon batter into prepared pan. Bake 1-1/2 to 1-3/4 hours, until a skewer inserted into center of cake comes out clean.

Cool cake in pan 5 minutes, then turn out onto a wire rack to cool completely. In a saucepan, gently heat honey. Brush over cake and arrange fruits and angelica on top.

Makes 8 to 10 slices.

Variation: A traditional Madeira cake has thin sliced candied peel on top. This should be placed on cake after it has been baking about 1 hour.

— COCONUT & CHERRY CAKE —

1 cup butter, softened
1-1/4 cups sugar
4 eggs and 1 egg yolk
2 cups self-rising flour, sifted
2/3 cup shredded coconut
1 cup candied cherries, quartered
TOPPING:
1 egg white
1/2 cup powdered sugar, sifted
1-1/4 cups unsweetened thin coconut slices

Preheat oven to 350F (175C). Grease an 8-inch springform cake pan and line with waxed paper.

In a bowl, beat butter and sugar until light and fluffy. In another bowl, beat together eggs and egg yolk. Gradually beat into creamed mixture. Fold in flour, coconut and cherries. Spoon mixture into prepared pan. Bake 45 to 50 minutes, until just firm to the touch. To make the topping, in a bowl, beat egg white until soft peaks form; gradually beat in powdered sugar until stiff peaks form.

Spread topping over top of cake. Sprinkle with coconut. Return cake to oven and bake 20 minutes, until golden-brown and a skewer inserted into center comes out clean. Cover lightly with foil if topping is browning too quickly. Cool cake in pan 10 minutes, then remove from pan, peel off lining paper and transfer to a wire rack to cool.

Makes 8 to 10 slices.

Note: Thin, dried slices of unsweetened coconut are available in natural food stores.

DUNDEE CAKE

1 cup butter, softened
1-1/2 cups packed brown sugar
4 eggs, beaten
2-1/2 cups all-purpose flour, sifted
1/4 cup milk
1/2 cup ground blanched almonds
3/4 cup dried currants
3/4 cup golden raisins
3/4 cup dark raisins
1/3 cup chopped mixed candied citrus peel
1/3 cup candied cherries, halved
Grated zests of 1 small orange and 1 small lemon
1/2 teaspoon baking soda, dissolved in 1 teaspoon milk
1/3 cup whole blanched almonds

Preheat oven to 325F (165C). Grease and line an 8-inch springform cake pan with waxed paper. In a bowl, beat butter and sugar until light and fluffy. Gradually beat in eggs. Fold in flour alternately with milk. Carefully fold in ground almonds, currants, golden raisins, raisins, peel, cherries and orange and lemon zests. Add baking soda dissolved in milk. Stir to mix.

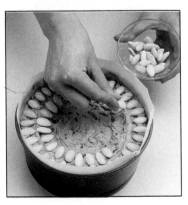

Pour batter into prepared pan. Smooth top with a metal spatula. Arrange blanched almonds in concentric circles over top of cake. Bake 2-1/2 to 3 hours, until a skewer inserted into center of the cake comes out clean. Cool in pan 30 minutes, then turn out cake, peel off lining paper and transfer to a wire rack to cool completely.

Makes about 12 slices.

—— APPLE STREUSEL CAKE ——

1-1/2 cups self-rising flour
1 teaspoon baking powder
1/2 cup margarine, softened
1/2 cup sugar
2 eggs, beaten
1 or 2 tablespoons milk
TOPPING:
1 cup self-rising flour
1 teaspoon ground cinnamon
6 tablespoons butter
1/3 cup granulated sugar
1 pound Granny Smith apples
A little lemon juice
Powdered sugar, to finish

Preheat oven to 350F (175C). Grease a 9-inch springform pan. To make topping, into a bowl, sift flour and cinnamon. Cut in butter until mixture resembles coarse crumbs. Stir in granulated sugar; set aside. Peel, core and thinly slice apples. Toss in a little lemon juice.

In another bowl, sift flour and baking powder. Add margarine, sugar and eggs. Beat well until mixture is smooth, adding just enough milk to make a good consistency. Spoon into prepared pan. Cover with apple slices and sprinkle with streusel topping. Bake 1 hour, until firm to the touch and golden-brown. Cool in pan before opening sides. Dust with powdered sugar.

Makes 8 to 10 slices.

Note: Keep cake 24 hours before serving.

HONEY SPICE CAKE

2/3 cup butter or margarine
3/4 cup packed light brown sugar
1/2 cup honey
1 tablespoon water
1-3/4 cups self-rising flour
1-1/2 teaspoons apple pie spice
2 eggs, beaten
FROSTING:
2-1/4 cups powdered sugar
About 3 tablespoons water

Preheat oven to 350F (175C). Grease a fluted ring mold with a 3-3/4-cup capacity. Into a saucepan, put butter, sugar, honey and water.

Heat gently until butter has melted and sugar has dissolved. Remove from heat and cool 10 minutes. Into a bowl, sift flour and apple pie spice. Pour in melted mixture and eggs; beat well until smooth. Pour batter into prepared pan. Bake 40 to 50 minutes, until well risen and a skewer inserted into center comes out clean. Cool cake in pan 2 to 3 minutes, then turn out cake and transfer to a wire rack to cool completely.

To make frosting, into a bowl, sift powdered sugar. Stir in enough water to make a smooth frosting. Carefully spoon frosting over cake so cake is evenly covered.

Makes 8 to 10 slices.

—CHOCOLATE MARBLE CAKE—

2 ounces semisweet chocolate
1 tablespoon strong coffee
2 cups self-rising flour
1 teaspoon baking powder
1 cup margarine, softened
1-1/4 cups sugar
4 eggs, beaten
1/2 cup ground blanched almonds
2 tablespoons milk
FROSTING:
4-1/2 ounces semisweet chocolate
2 tablespoons butter
2 tablespoons water

Preheat oven to 350F (175C). Grease a ring mold with a 7-1/2-cup capacity. In a heat-proof bowl set over a pan of simmering water, break chocolate and add coffee. Heat until melted. Let cool. Into a bowl, sift flour and baking powder. Add margarine, sugar, eggs, ground almonds and milk. Beat well until smooth. Spoon half the batter evenly into prepared pan. Stir cooled, soft chocolate into the remaining batter, then spoon into pan. Draw a knife through batter in a spiral. Smooth the surface.

Bake 50 to 60 minutes, until well risen and a skewer inserted into center comes out clean. Cool in pan 5 minutes, then turn out cake and transfer to a wire rack to cool completely. To make frosting, into a heatproof bowl set over a pan of simmering water, put choco-late, butter and water; heat until melted. Stir frosting and pour over cake on a rack, work-ing quickly to coat top and sides. Let set before serving.

Makes 10 to 12 slices.

TOFFEE DATE CAKE

1-2/3 cups chopped dates
1-1/4 cups boiling water
1/2 cup butter, softened
3/4 cup sugar
3 eggs, beaten
2 cups self-rising flour, sifted
1/2 teaspoon ground cinnamon
1 teaspoon baking soda
1 teaspoon vanilla extract
TOPPING:
1/2 cup packed brown sugar
1/4 cup butter
3 tablespoons whipping cream

Cover dates with the boiling water.

Preheat oven to 350F (175C). Grease a 9-inch springform pan. In a bowl, beat butter and sugar until light and fluffy. Gradually beat in eggs. Fold in flour and cinnamon. Add baking soda and vanilla to dates and water. Pour onto creamed mixture; stir until thoroughly mixed. Pour into prepared pan. Bake 1 to 1-1/4 hours, until well risen and firm to the touch. Meanwhile, preheat broiler.

To make topping, into a saucepan, put brown sugar, butter and cream. Heat gently until sugar is melted. Bring to a boil, then simmer 3 minutes. Pour topping over cake and put under the broiler until topping is bubbling. Cool in pan until toffee is set. Turn out cake, then transfer to a wire rack to cool completely.

Makes 8 to 10 slices.

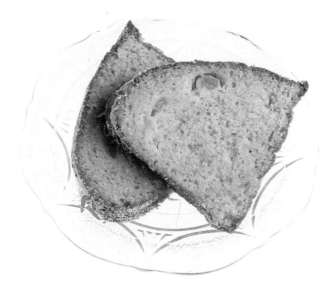

—— PEACH & ORANGE CAKE ——

1/2 cup canned peach slices
3/4 cup butter
1-1/4 cups sugar
Grated zest of 1 orange
4 eggs, beaten
2/3 cup dairy sour cream
2 cups all-purpose flour
1/2 teaspoon baking soda
TO FINISH:
Powdered sugar
Grated zest of 1 orange

Preheat oven to 350F (175C). Grease a kugelhopf mold and dust with flour. Drain peach slices and coarsely chop.

In a bowl, beat butter and sugar until light and fluffy. Add orange zest and gradually beat in eggs. Fold in peaches and sour cream. Sift flour and baking soda onto batter. Fold in gently and spread into prepared pan, smoothing the top with a metal spatula. Bake 45 to 50 minutes, until well risen and golden-brown.

Cool in pan 10 minutes, then turn out cake and transfer to a wire rack to cool completely. Sift powdered sugar over cake. Decorate with orange zest.

Makes 8 to 10 slices.

—BLACK CURRANT WHIRLS—

1 cup butter, softened
1/3 cup powdered sugar, sifted
few drops almond extract
2 cups all-purpose flour
2 tablespoons black currant jam
TO FINISH:
Powdered sugar for dusting

Preheat oven to 350F (175C). Arrange 12 paper cupcake cups in a muffin pan. In a bowl, beat butter with powdered sugar and almond extract until creamy. Sift flour onto mixture and beat until smooth.

Spoon batter into a pastry bag fitted with a large star tip. Pipe whirls into paper cups, covering bottoms. Pipe a ring around edge to leave a slight hollow in center.

Bake 20 minutes, until set and very lightly browned. Transfer from muffin pan to a wire rack to cool. Put a little jam in center of each whirl. Dust lightly with powdered sugar.

Makes 12.

STRAWBERRY-ROSE MERINGUES

MERINGUES:
2 egg whites
1/2 cup sugar
FILLING:
2/3 cup whipping cream
4 medium-size strawberries
2 teaspoons powdered sugar
2 teaspoons rosewater
TO DECORATE:
12 strawberries

Preheat oven to 250F (120C). Line 2 baking sheets with parchment paper.

To make meringues, in a bowl, beat egg whites until soft peaks form. Slowly beat in sugar until stiff peaks form. Spoon meringue into a pastry bag fitted with a large star tip. Pipe 24 (3-inch) strips onto prepared baking sheets. Bake 1 hour, until dry and crisp. Cool on wire racks.

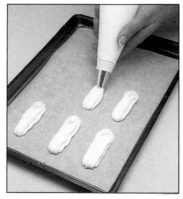

To make filling, in a bowl, whip cream until stiff peaks form. In a food processor or blender, process strawberries until smooth. Press through a strainer into a bowl. Stir in powdered sugar and rosewater. Add cream and mix well together. Sandwich meringues together with strawberry cream. Decorate with strawberries and serve at once.

Makes 12.

HONEY MADELEINES

1/4 cup butter
2 eggs
1/4 cup sugar
1 tablespoon honey
1/2 cup all-purpose flour
1/2 teaspoon baking powder
TO FINISH:
Powdered sugar for sifting

Preheat oven to 375F (190C). Lightly butter 12 madeleine molds. In a small saucepan over low heat, melt the 1/4 cup butter. Cool.

In a bowl, beat eggs and sugar until pale and thick. Stir in melted butter and honey. Sift flour and baking powder onto egg mixture, then fold in.

Spoon mixture into prepared molds. Bake 10 minutes, until light golden-brown. Leave in molds 2 minutes, then turn out and transfer to a wire rack to cool. Dust lightly with powdered sugar.

Makes 12.

Note: If you do not have madeleine molds, these light cakes can be made in tartlet pans.

── CHOCOLATE BROWNIES ──

1/2 cup all-purpose flour
1/4 cup unsweetened cocoa powder
1/2 cup butter
1-1/4 cups sugar
1 teaspoon vanilla extract
2 eggs, beaten
1/2 cup chopped walnuts
FROSTING:
4 ounces semisweet chocolate
2/3 cup dairy sour cream

Preheat oven to 325F (165C). Butter an 8-inch square cake pan. Onto a plate, sift flour and cocoa powder.

Into a saucepan over low heat, put butter, sugar and 1 tablespoon cold water. Stir until butter melts. Remove from heat. Stir in vanilla, then beat in eggs, one at a time. Add flour and cocoa powder and beat to a smooth, shiny batter. Stir in walnuts. Pour batter into prepared pan. Bake 20 minutes, until set. Leave in pan to cool completely.

To make frosting, into a heatproof bowl over a pan of simmering water, break chocolate. Heat until chocolate is melted. Stir until smooth, then remove from heat. Stir in sour cream and beat until evenly blended. Spoon topping over brownies and make a swirling pattern with a spatula. Leave in a cool place to set. Cut into squares and remove from pan.

Makes 9 large or 16 small brownies.

— STRAWBERRY SHORTCAKE —

2 cups all-purpose flour
1 tablespoon baking powder
5 teaspoons sugar
1/3 cup butter, chilled
1/3 cup milk
FILLING:
1-1/2 pounds strawberries
1/4 cup sugar
1-1/4 cups whipping cream

Preheat oven to 425F (220C). Grease a baking sheet. Into a bowl, sift flour and baking powder.

Stir in sugar. Cut in butter until mixture resembles bread crumbs. Pour in milk and mix to form a soft dough. Turn out dough onto a lightly floured surface, then roll out to 1/4 inch thick. Cut into 8 (3-inch) circles. Place on prepared baking sheet. Bake 10 to 12 minutes, until golden-brown. Slice most of strawberries, reserving a few for decoration. In a bowl, mix together sliced strawberries and sugar. In another bowl, whip cream until soft peaks form.

Split shortcakes in half while still warm. Spread bottom halves with two-thirds of the cream. Cover cream with sliced strawberries and top with other shortcake halves. Add a swirl of cream to each one and decorate with reserved strawberries.

Makes 8.

CHERRY-NUT ROCKS

2/3 cup candied cherries
1/2 cup walnuts
2 cups all-purpose flour
2 teaspoons baking powder
1/2 teaspoon apple pie spice
1 cup packed brown sugar
3/4 cup butter, chilled
1 egg, beaten
1 to 2 tablespoons milk (optional)

Preheat oven to 375F (190C). Grease a baking sheet. With a sharp knife, cut cherries into quarters. Coarsely chop walnuts.

Into a bowl, sift flour, baking powder and apple pie spice. Stir in sugar. Cut in butter until mixture resembles bread crumbs. Stir in cherries and nuts. Stir egg into flour mixture to form a stiff dough. Add a little milk, if necessary.

Using 2 forks, pile the mixture in rocky heaps on prepared baking sheet. Bake 15 to 20 minutes, until golden-brown and firm to the touch. Cool on baking sheet 2 minutes, then, using a metal spatula, transfer to a wire rack to cool completely.

Makes 10 to 12.

SPONGE DROPS

1/2 cup all-purpose flour
2 large eggs
1/4 cup sugar
Sugar for sprinkling
FILLING:
2/3 cup whipping cream
4 teaspoons red jam

Preheat oven to 375F (190C). Grease several baking sheets and line with waxed paper. Into a bowl, sift flour. In another bowl, beat together eggs and sugar until pale and thick.

Sift flour again onto egg mixture, then fold in very gently. Spoon batter into a pastry bag fitted with a 1-inch plain tip. Pipe batter onto prepared baking sheets in 1-1/2-inch circles. Sprinkle each circle with sugar. Bake 10 minutes, until light golden. Slide paper with sponge drops still attached off baking sheet onto a damp dish towel. Cool completely.

In a bowl, whip cream until stiff peaks form. Remove sponge drops from paper. Sandwich together in pairs with a little jam and whipped cream.

Makes 18.

——— GINGER BRANDY SNAPS ———

1/4 cup unsalted butter
1/4 cup packed dark brown sugar
2 tablespoons light corn syrup
1/2 cup all-purpose flour
1/2 teaspoon ground ginger
1 teaspoon brandy
FILLING:
1-1/4 cups whipping cream
1 tablespoon stem ginger syrup
6 pieces stem ginger

Preheat oven to 350F (175C).

Grease several baking sheets. Butter the handles of 3 or 4 wooden spoons. Into a saucepan over medium heat, put butter, brown sugar and syrup. Heat until butter melts. Cool slightly. Sift flour and ginger onto melted ingredients and stir in with brandy. Drop teaspoonfuls of mixture, well spaced out, onto baking sheets. Bake 7 to 10 minutes, until brandy snaps are golden.

Quickly remove brandy snaps from baking sheets and roll around spoon handles, leaving them in place until set. Slide off spoons and leave on wire racks until completely cool. In a bowl, beat cream with ginger syrup until stiff peaks form. Spoon cream into a pastry bag fitted with a small star tip. Pipe into each end of brandy snaps. Slice stem ginger pieces and use to decorate brandy snaps. Refrigerate until ready to serve.

Makes about 18.

QUEEN CAKES

1/3 cup dried currants
1 cup self-rising flour
1/4 cup butter, softened
1/4 cup sugar
1 egg
Finely shredded zest of 1 lemon
1 tablespoon whipping cream

Preheat oven to 350F (175C). Thoroughly butter 9 individual brioche molds. Put currants into bottoms of molds. Stand molds on a baking sheet.

Into a bowl, sift flour, then set aside. In another bowl, beat butter and sugar until creamy. Mix together egg and lemon zest, then gradually beat into creamed mixture. Add half the flour and fold in lightly. Add remaining flour and the whipping cream and mix to a smooth consistency.

Spoon batter into brioche molds on top of currants. Bake 15 to 20 minutes, until golden. Turn out of molds while still hot. Leave on a wire rack to cool completely. Serve currant sides up.

Makes 9.

Note: If you do not have brioche molds, use paper cupcake cups placed in muffin pans.

– LEMON BUTTERFLY CUPCAKES –

1/3 cup butter, softened
1/3 cup sugar
1 egg, beaten
1 cup self-rising flour
Shredded zest of 1/2 lemon
3 to 6 tablespoons milk
FROSTING:
1/4 cup butter, softened
3/4 cup powdered sugar, sifted
1 tablespoon lemon juice
TO DECORATE:
A few black and green grapes

Preheat oven to 375F (190C). Put 12 paper cupcake cups into a muffin pan.

In a bowl, beat butter and sugar until creamy. Gradually add egg to creamed mixture, beating well after each addition. Add half of the flour and the lemon zest and fold in lightly. Add remaining flour and enough milk to make a thick batter. Spoon mixture into paper cups. Bake 15 to 20 minutes, until well risen and brown. Cool on a wire rack.

When cupcakes are cool, cut a shallow cone from center of each one; reserve. To make frosting, in a bowl, beat together butter and powdered sugar until creamy. Add lemon juice and beat until smooth and well blended. Fill hollow in top of each cupcake with frosting. Cut the reserved cones in half and arrange in frosting to resemble wings. Cut grapes into quarters and use them to decorate cupcakes.

Makes 12.

SUMMER CAKE

3/4 cup butter, softened
3/4 cup sugar
3 eggs, beaten
1-1/2 cups self-rising flour
4 teaspoons boiling water
FILLING:
1/3 cup unsalted butter, softened
3/4 cup powdered sugar, sifted
1 teaspoon vanilla extract
FROSTING:
1 cup powdered sugar, sifted
2 teaspoons lemon juice
TO DECORATE:
Crystallized flowers

Preheat oven to 350F (175C). Grease two 8-inch round cake pans and line bottoms with waxed paper. In a bowl, beat together butter and sugar until light and fluffy. Gradually beat in eggs, then fold in flour. Stir in the boiling water to make a soft batter. Divide batter between prepared pans. Bake 25 to 30 minutes, until cakes are lightly browned and spring back when pressed. Cool in pans 5 minutes, then turn out cakes, peel off lining paper and transfer to wire racks to cool.

To make filling, in a bowl, beat together butter and powdered sugar. Stir in vanilla. Sandwich cakes together with filling. To make icing, in a bowl, mix together powdered sugar, lemon juice and enough water to make a good consistency for spreading. Spread frosting over cake top and decorate with crystallized flowers.

Makes 8 slices.

——— STRAWBERRY ROULADE ———

6 eggs
1 cup sugar
2 teaspoons baking powder
1-2/3 cups ground blanched almonds
FILLING:
2/3 cup cream cheese (5 ounces), softened
2/3 cup whipping cream
1/2 pound strawberries
2 passion fruit
TO DECORATE:
Powdered sugar
A few whole strawberries

Preheat oven to 350F (175C). Grease a 15" × 10" jellyroll pan and line with waxed paper.

Separate eggs. In a bowl, beat whites until stiff but not dry. In another bowl, beat together egg yolks and sugar until pale and thick. Mix baking powder thoroughly into ground almonds. Stir gently into yolk mixture, without overmixing. Carefully fold in egg whites. Spread batter in pan. Bake 15 minutes, until firm. Cover with a towel and leave cake to cool in pan.

In a bowl, beat cream cheese and cream until soft peaks form. Reserve one-third. Mash half of the strawberries; chop remaining strawberries. Scoop out passion fruit flesh and stir into cream with mashed strawberries. Place a sheet of waxed paper on a flat surface; dust thickly with powdered sugar. Turn roulade out onto paper. Peel off lining paper. Spread cream over roulade; sprinkle with chopped strawberries. Roll up and pipe reserved cream on top. Decorate with reserved strawberries.

Makes 6 to 8 servings.

– DOUBLE CHOCOLATE GÂTEAU –

1 cup butter, softened
1-1/4 cups sugar
4 eggs, beaten
1-1/2 cups self-rising flour
1/2 cup unsweetened cocoa powder
FILLING:
1 cup whipping cream
5 ounces white chocolate
FROSTING:
12 ounces semisweet chocolate
1/2 cup butter
6 tablespoons whipping cream
TO DECORATE:
4 ounces semisweet chocolate
2 teaspoons each powdered sugar and unsweetened
   cocoa powder mixed

To make the filling, in a saucepan, heat cream to just below boiling point. In a food processor, chop white chocolate. With motor running, pour hot cream through feed tube and process 10 to 15 seconds, until smooth. Transfer to a bowl, cover with plastic wrap and chill overnight. The next day after cake is ready to fill, beat filling until just beginning to hold soft peaks.

To make chocolate curls for decoration, in a heatproof bowl over a pan of simmering water, melt chocolate. Spread one-quarter of chocolate over a baking sheet. Refrigerate sheet a few minutes until chocolate loses its gloss and is just set, but not hard. Using a metal spatula, scrape off large curls of chocolate, transferring them to a baking sheet lined with waxed paper. Refrigerate until set. Make 3 more batches of curls in the same way.

Preheat oven to 350F (175C). Grease an 8-inch springform cake pan and line bottom with waxed paper. In a bowl, beat together butter and sugar until light and fluffy. Gradually beat in eggs. Into another bowl, sift together flour and cocoa powder. Fold into mixture, then spoon into pan. Bake 45 to 50 minutes, until cake springs back when lightly pressed and a skewer inserted into center comes out clean. Cool in pan 5 minutes, then turn out cake, remove lining paper and transfer to a wire rack to cool completely.

To make frosting, in a heatproof bowl over a pan of simmering water, melt chocolate. Stir in butter and cream. Cool, stirring occasionally, until mixture is a thick spreading consistency.

With a serrated knife, slice the cake horizontally into 3 layers. Sandwich layers together with white chocolate filling. Cover top and sides of cake with chocolate frosting. Arrange chocolate curls over top of cake. Sift mixed powdered sugar and cocoa powder over cake.

Makes 10 slices.

—CHOC-ALMOND MERINGUE—

MERINGUE:
4 egg whites
1-1/4 cups sugar
1-1/4 cups ground blanched almonds
FILLING:
6 ounces semisweet chocolate
3 tablespoons unsalted butter
3 tablespoons strong coffee
3 tablespoons brandy
3/4 cup whipping cream
TO DECORATE:
Chopped, toasted almonds

Preheat oven to 275F (80C). Line 2 baking sheets with waxed paper.

To make meringue, in a bowl, beat egg whites until soft peaks form. Beat in half of the sugar until stiff peaks form. In another bowl, mix together remaining sugar and ground almonds. Carefully fold into meringue mixture. Pipe or spread meringue into 2 (8-inch) circles on prepared baking sheets. Bake about 1-1/2 hours, until completely dry and crisp. Carefully remove from baking sheets and transfer to wire racks to cool completely.

To make filling, into a heatproof bowl set over a pan of simmering water, break chocolate. Add butter, coffee and brandy. When melted, stir and set aside to cool. Whip cream until soft peaks form; stir in cooled chocolate mixture. Sandwich meringue circles together with most of the chocolate cream. Put remaining cream into a pastry bag and pipe whirls on top of cake. Decorate with toasted almonds.

Makes 8 servings.

FROSTED WALNUT CAKE

3/4 cup butter, softened
3/4 cup sugar
3 eggs, beaten
1/2 cup chopped walnuts
1-1/2 cups self-rising flour, sifted
FROSTING:
1-1/4 cups sugar
1/3 cup water
2 egg whites
6 walnut halves

Preheat oven to 350F (175C). Grease 2 (8-inch) round cake pans and line bottoms with waxed paper. In a bowl, beat together butter and sugar until light and fluffy.

Gradually beat in eggs. Fold in walnuts and flour. Divide batter between prepared pans. Bake 25 to 35 minutes, until risen and golden-brown. Cool in pans 5 minutes, then turn out cakes, peel off lining papers and transfer to wire racks to cool. To make frosting, in a saucepan, put sugar and 1/3 cup water. Stir over low heat until sugar has dissolved.

Bring to a boil and boil to 240F (115C) on a candy thermometer. Remove from heat. In a bowl, beat egg whites until stiff peaks form. Pour hot syrup onto egg whites, beating constantly. Continue beating as mixture cools. Use some frosting to sandwich cakes together; cover cake with remaining frosting. Decorate with walnut halves. Let frosting set overnight.

Makes 8 servings.

—— PINEAPPLE-CARROT CAKE ——

1-3/4 cups lightly packed grated carrots
1 cup walnuts
1 (15-oz.) can crushed pineapple
1 cup packed light brown sugar
3 eggs
2-1/2 cups all-purpose flour
1 teaspoon baking soda
2 teaspoons baking powder
3/4 cup vegetable oil
1/2 cup cream cheese (4 ounces), softened
1/4 cup butter, softened
1 cup powdered sugar
1 teaspoon vanilla extract
TO DECORATE:
Candied pineapple

Preheat oven to 350F (175C). Grease a 9-inch springform cake pan and line bottom with waxed paper. Add carrots to a bowl. Chop walnuts; add to carrots. Drain pineapple and add to bowl with sugar and eggs. Sift flour, baking soda and baking powder into bowl. Add oil and beat thoroughly until blended. Pour into pan. Bake 50 to 60 minutes, until well risen and a skewer inserted into center comes out clean.

Cool cake in pan 5 minutes, then turn out cake and transfer to a wire rack to cool completely. To make frosting, in a bowl, beat together cream cheese, butter, powdered sugar and vanilla until smooth. Spread over cake. Decorate with candied pineapple.

Makes 10 to 12 servings.

— CHOCOLATE-ORANGE CAKE —

2 small oranges
3 ounces semisweet chocolate
1-3/4 cups self-rising flour
1-1/2 teaspoons baking powder
3/4 cup margarine, softened
3/4 cup sugar
3 eggs, beaten
TO GLAZE:
1-1/2 cups powdered sugar
2 tablespoons orange juice
2 ounces semisweet chocolate

Preheat oven to 325F (165C). Thoroughly grease a fluted or plain ring mold with a 3-3/4-cup capacity.

With a sharp knife, cut peel and pith from oranges. Cut oranges into sections by cutting down between membranes. Chop sections into small pieces, reserving as much juice as possible. Grate chocolate coarsely. Into a bowl, sift flour and baking powder. Add margarine, sugar, eggs and any reserved orange juice. Beat thoroughly until batter is smooth. Fold in chopped oranges and grated chocolate. Spoon batter into prepared mold.

Bake 40 minutes, until well risen and golden-brown. Cool in mold 5 minutes, then turn out cake and transfer to a wire rack to cool completely. To make frosting, into a bowl, sift powdered sugar. Stir in enough orange juice to make a thin frosting. Using a spoon, drizzle frosting over cake. Into a heatproof bowl over a pan of simmering water, break chocolate. Melt. Drizzle chocolate over cake. Let set.

Makes 8 to 10 slices.

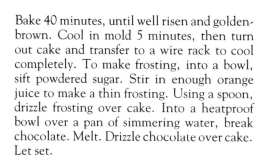

—— LEMON MOUSSE GÂTEAU ——

CAKE:
3 eggs
1/2 cup plus 1 tablespoon sugar
1 teaspoon vanilla extract
3/4 cup all-purpose flour
FILLING:
Grated zest and juice of 2 lemons
2 teaspoons unflavored gelatin powder
3 eggs, separated
1/2 cup sugar
2/3 cup whipping cream
TO DECORATE:
Powdered sugar
Raspberries
Lemon geranium or raspberry leaves, if available

Preheat oven to 350F (175C). Grease a 9-inch springform pan and line with waxed paper. To make cake, in a bowl, beat eggs and sugar together until very thick and light. Stir in vanilla, then sift flour onto mixture and fold in gently. Spoon into prepared pan and bake 25 minutes, until golden and the cake springs back when lightly pressed. Turn cake out onto a wire rack covered with sugared waxed paper. Peel off lining paper and cool completely.

With a serrated knife, slice the cake horizontally into 2 layers. Wash and dry cake pan and line bottom and sides with waxed paper. Place 1 cake layer in bottom of pan.

To make mousse filling, into a bowl, put juice of 1 lemon and 1 tablespoon water. Sprinkle with gelatin. Let stand 10 minutes to soften. In a bowl, beat together egg yolks, sugar and lemon zest until thick. Gradually beat in remaining lemon juice, keeping mixture as thick as possible.

Place bowl of gelatin over a pan of simmering water until gelatin has dissolved. Immediately beat it into egg-yolk mixture. In a bowl, whip cream until it just holds its shape. Fold cream into egg mixture. Beat egg whites until stiff but not dry. Gently fold into mousse. Pour mixture into prepared pan. Level surface. Cover and refrigerate 45 to 60 minutes, until lightly set. Place second layer of cake on top. Cover and refrigerate overnight.

To serve, remove sides of pan and carefully peel away paper. Place a flat plate on top of cake and quickly invert cake. Ease off bottom of pan. Dust cake with sifted powdered sugar and decorate with raspberries and geranium or raspberry leaves, if using.

Makes 8 to 10 servings.

──COFFEE-CARAMEL CAKE──

2 cups self-rising flour
3/4 cup butter, softened
3/4 cup sugar
3 eggs, beaten
7 tablespoons strong coffee
FROSTING AND DECORATION:
1/2 cup half and half
3/4 cup plus 1 tablespoon butter
3 tablespoons sugar
3-3/4 cups powdered sugar
Chocolate-covered coffee beans

Preheat oven to 350F (175C). Grease 2 (8-inch) round cake pans and line the bottoms with waxed paper.

Into a bowl, sift flour 3 times and set aside. In another bowl, beat together butter and sugar until light and fluffy. Gradually beat in eggs. Fold in flour alternately with coffee. Divide batter between prepared pans and bake 30 minutes, until slightly shrinking from sides of pans. Cool cakes in pans 5 minutes, then turn out cakes and transfer to wire racks to cool completely. To make frosting, in a saucepan, warm half and half and butter.

In another heavy-bottomed saucepan, heat sugar over low heat until it dissolves and turns a golden caramel. Off the heat, stir in warm half and half mixture, taking care as it may splatter. Return to the heat and stir until caramel has dissolved. Remove from heat. Gradually stir in powdered sugar, beating until frosting is a smooth spreading consistency. Sandwich cakes together with some frosting; spread remaining frosting over top and side. Decorate with coffee beans.

Makes 8 servings.

——TIA MARIA CHOUX RING——

1 recipe Choux Pastry (page 84)
2 tablespoons all-purpose flour
2 tablespoons cornstarch
1/4 cup sugar
1-1/4 cups milk
3 egg yolks
2/3 cup whipping cream
1/2 teaspoon coffee extract
2-1/4 teaspoons Tia Maria
3/4 cup powdered sugar, sifted

Preheat oven to 425F (220C). Spoon pastry into a pastry bag fitted with a 1/2-inch plain tip.

Pipe a double 8-inch circle onto a paper-lined baking sheet. Bake choux ring 20 minutes. Reduce temperature to 350F (175C) and bake 10 to 15 minutes longer, until golden-brown. Split horizontally, then cool on a wire rack. Into a bowl, sift flour and cornstarch. Stir in sugar and 2 tablespoons milk to make a thick paste. Beat in egg yolks. In a saucepan, heat remaining milk to just below boiling point. Pour onto egg mixture, stirring constantly.

Strain mixture back into saucepan, then cook over low heat, stirring constantly, until thickened. Cover closely with plastic wrap and refrigerate until chilled. In a bowl, whip cream until stiff peaks form and fold into custard. Stir in 2 teaspoons of the coffee extract and Tia Maria. Sandwich choux rings together with coffee filling. In a bowl, mix together powdered sugar, remaining 1/4 teaspoon coffee extract and about 1 tablespoon water. Spoon over cake and let set.

Makes 8 servings.

MAIDS OF HONOR

1-1/2 recipes Pie Crust Dough (page 89)
1/2 cup cottage cheese
1/4 cup butter, softened
1/4 cup sugar
Shredded zest and juice of 1/2 lemon
1/4 cup ground blanched almonds
1/2 teaspoon grated nutmeg
2 teaspoons brandy
1/3 cup dried currants
TO FINISH:
Sugar for sprinkling

Roll out pastry and use to line 12 tartlet pans. Refrigerate 30 minutes.

Preheat oven to 375F (190C). Press cottage cheese through a strainer into a bowl. Add butter and beat until well blended. Add sugar, lemon zest and juice, ground almonds, nutmeg and brandy. Mix thoroughly. Stir in currants.

Spoon batter into prepared dough cases. Bake 20 to 30 minutes, until risen and golden-brown. Sprinkle with sugar. Transfer to a wire rack to cool.

Makes 12.

PALMIERS

1/2 pound puff pastry dough, thawed if frozen
1/4 cup sugar, plus extra for rolling out
FILLING:
1/2 cup whipping cream
4 teaspoons red jelly (such as red currant jelly)

Preheat oven to 425F (220C). On a surface sprinkled with sugar, roll out dough to a 12-inch square. Sprinkle dough with half of the sugar. Fold sides of dough into center, sprinkle with half of remaining sugar, then fold sides into center again.

Sprinkle dough with remaining sugar and fold in half down center. Press lightly together to seal the edges. Cut dough into 24 slices. Place slices, cut edges down, on dampened baking sheets. With palm of your hand, press to flatten slightly. Bake 10 minutes, or until crisp and a light golden-brown. Turn over and bake 2 to 3 minutes more, until second side is golden-brown. Remove from baking sheets immediately and cool on wire racks.

In a bowl, whip cream until soft peaks form. Spread a little jelly on 12 of the palmiers. Spread cream over jelly, then top with remaining 12 palmiers.

Makes 12.

RASPBERRY ECLAIRS

CHOUX PASTRY:
1/2 cup unsalted butter
2/3 cup water
1/3 cup all-purpose flour, sifted
2 eggs, beaten
FILLING:
3/4 cup whipping cream
1 tablespoon powdered sugar
6 ounces raspberries
FROSTING:
3/4 cup powdered sugar, sifted
2 teaspoons lemon juice
Pink food coloring (optional)

Preheat oven to 425F (220C). Into a sauce-pan, put butter and water, and bring to a boil. Add flour all at once and beat thoroughly until mixture leaves the side of the pan. Cool slightly, then vigorously beat in eggs, one at a time. Spoon dough into a pastry bag fitted with a plain 1/2-inch tip and pipe 20 to 24 (3-inch) strips onto dampened baking sheets. Bake 10 minutes. Reduce temperature to 375F (190C); bake 20 minutes more, until golden.

Slit the side of each eclair, then leave on wire racks to cool. To make filling, in a bowl, whip cream and powdered sugar until stiff peaks form. Put into a pastry bag fitted with a 1/8-inch tip. Pipe the filling into each eclair. Put a few raspberries in each eclair. To make frosting, in a small bowl, mix powdered sugar with lemon juice and enough water to make a smooth paste. Add pink coloring, if desired. Spread frosting over eclairs and let set.

Makes 20 to 24.

—— SUMMER FRUIT TARTLETS ——

1-3/4 cups all-purpose flour, sifted
1/2 cup ground blanched almonds
1/2 cup powdered sugar, sifted
1/2 cup butter, chilled
1 egg yolk
1 tablespoon milk
FILLING:
1 cup cream cheese (8 ounces), softened
Sugar, to taste
3/4 pound fresh summer fruits, such as red and black
  currants, raspberries and wild strawberries
Red currant jelly or other red jelly, heated, to glaze

In a bowl, mix together flour, ground almonds and powdered sugar. Cut in butter until mixture resembles bread crumbs. Add egg yolk and milk; work in with a spatula, then with fingers until dough binds together. Wrap dough in plastic wrap and refrigerate 30 minutes. Preheat oven to 400F (205C). On a floured surface, roll out dough to about 1/8 inch thick. Line 12 deep tartlet pans or individual brioche molds with dough; prick bottoms.

Press a piece of foil into each dough case, covering the edges. Bake 10 to 15 minutes, until light golden-brown. Remove foil and bake 2 to 3 minutes longer. Transfer to a wire rack to cool. To make filling, in a bowl, mix cream cheese and sugar together. Put a spoonful of filling in each pastry shell. Arrange fruit on top, then brush with glaze and serve at once.

Makes 12.

——MAPLE-PECAN TARTLETS——

1-1/4 cups all-purpose flour
1/3 cup butter, chilled
3 tablespoons powdered sugar
1 egg yolk
1 teaspoon lemon juice
FILLING:
2 tablespoons maple syrup
2/3 cup whipping cream
1/2 cup sugar
Pinch of cream of tartar
1 cup chopped pecans
Pecan halves

To make dough, into a bowl, sift flour. Cut in butter until mixture resembles bread crumbs.

Stir in powdered sugar. Add egg yolk, lemon juice and about 1 teaspoon water to form a firm dough. Turn dough out onto a lightly floured surface. Knead lightly. Wrap in plastic wrap and refrigerate 30 minutes. Pre-heat oven to 400F (205C). On a lightly floured surface, roll out dough to about 1/8 inch thick. Line 14 tartlet pans with dough; prick bottoms. Press a piece of foil into each dough case. Bake 10 to 15 minutes, until light golden-brown. Remove foil and bake 2 to 3 minutes longer. Transfer to a wire rack to cool.

To make filling, mix half the syrup with half the cream; set aside. In a pan, heat sugar, cream of tartar and 1/3 cup water until sugar dissolves. Bring to a boil; boil until light golden. Stir in maple syrup and cream mixture. Cook until mixture reaches 240F (115C) on a candy thermometer, or forms a soft ball when dropped in cold water. Stir in remaining cream. Cool slightly. Brush syrup over edges of tartlets. Put pecans in tartlets. Spoon over toffee. Top with halves.

Makes 14.

LEMON CUSTARD SLICES

1/2 pound puff pastry dough, thawed if frozen
FILLING:
3 tablespoons cornstarch
1/4 cup sugar
2/3 cup milk
Juice of 1 lemon
Shredded zest of 1/2 lemon
1 egg yolk
1/2 cup whipping cream
TO DECORATE:
1/2 cup powdered sugar, sifted
2 kiwifruit, peeled and sliced

Preheat oven to 450F (225C). On a lightly floured surface, roll out dough to a 12″ × 10″ rectangle. With a sharp, floured knife, cut dough into 8 rectangles. Prick all over with a fork. Place rectangles on a dampened baking sheet. Bake 10 to 15 minutes, until well risen and golden-brown. Transfer to a wire rack to cool. Split rectangles in half.

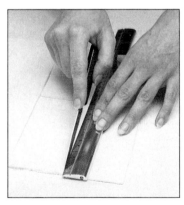

To make filling, in a saucepan, blend cornstarch with sugar and milk. Bring to a boil, stirring, until mixture thickens. Stir in lemon juice and zest. Beat in egg yolk. Cover and refrigerate until chilled. Beat in cream. In small bowl, mix powdered sugar with about 2 tablespoons water to make a smooth paste. Spread over 8 pastry slices. Let set. Spread custard over remaining pastry slices. Top with iced slices. Decorate with kiwifruit.

Makes 8.

NUTTY FILO FINGERS

1-1/4 cups skinned hazelnuts, very finely ground
1/4 cup granulated sugar
1 tablespoon orange-flower water
1/3 cup unsalted butter
6 large sheets filo pastry
TO FINISH:
Sugar for dusting

Preheat oven to 350F (175C). Grease 2 baking sheets. In a bowl, mix together ground hazelnuts, sugar and orange-flower water.

In a saucepan, melt butter. Cut each sheet of dough into 4 rectangles. Pile on top of each other and cover with a towel to prevent drying out. Working with 1 pile of dough rectangles at a time, brush each piece of dough with melted butter.

Spread 1 teaspoon of filling along a short end. Fold long sides in, folding slightly over filling. Roll up from filling end. Place on a prepared baking sheet with seam underneath. Brush with melted butter. Repeat with remaining pastry rectangles and filling. Bake 20 minutes, or until very lightly colored. Transfer to wire racks to cool; sprinkle with sugar.

Makes 24.

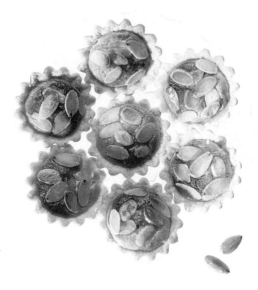

FRANGIPANE TARTLETS

PIE CRUST DOUGH:
1 cup all-purpose flour
Pinch of salt
1/4 cup butter or margarine, chilled
FILLING:
2 tablespoons apricot jam
1/4 cup butter, softened
1/4 cup sugar
1 egg
1/2 teaspoon almond extract
1 tablespoon all-purpose flour, sifted
1/2 cup ground blanched almonds
1/4 cup sliced almonds
GLAZE:
2 tablespoons apricot jam

Preheat oven to 375F (190C). Into a bowl, sift flour and salt. Cut in butter until mixture resembles bread crumbs. Add 1 or 2 tablespoons water to make a soft dough. On a floured surface, roll out dough about 1/8 inch thick. Line 12 tartlet pans with dough. Put a little apricot jam in bottom of each. To make filling, in a bowl, beat butter and sugar until creamy. Mix egg and almond extract together, then add to creamed mixture with flour and ground almonds. Mix well to form a smooth paste.

Spoon paste into dough cases. Arrange a few sliced almonds on top of each. Bake 15 to 20 minutes, until golden. To make glaze, in a saucepan, melt jam with 2 teaspoons cold water. Bring to a boil, then strain and reheat. Brush over hot tartlets. Transfer tartlets to a wire rack to cool.

Makes 12.

——ALMOND MACAROONS——

2 egg whites
3/4 cup ground blanched almonds
1/2 cup sugar
2 teaspoons cornstarch
1/4 teaspoon almond extract
12 blanched almond halves

Preheat oven to 350F (175C). Line 2 baking sheets with parchment paper or waxed paper. Reserve 2 teaspoons egg white. In a large bowl, put remaining egg whites and beat until soft peaks form.

Fold in ground almonds, sugar, cornstarch and almond extract until mixture is smooth. Put 6 spoonfuls of mixture onto each baking sheet and flatten slightly. Place an almond half in center of each macaroon. Brush lightly with reserved egg white.

Bake 20 minutes, until very lightly browned. Cool on baking sheets. When cold, remove macaroons from paper.

Makes 12.

LINZER HEARTS

1/2 cup butter, softened
1/4 cup sugar
1 egg, beaten
1/4 teaspoon almond extract
1-3/4 cups all-purpose flour
3 tablespoons cornstarch
1/2 teaspoon baking powder
FILLING:
6 tablespoons seedless raspberry jam
TO FINISH:
Powdered sugar for sifting

In a bowl, beat butter and sugar together until creamy. Gradually beat in egg, then beat in almond extract.

Into a bowl, sift flour, cornstarch and baking powder and blend together with a spoon, then work with your hands to form a soft dough. Cover with plastic wrap and refrigerate 30 minutes. Preheat oven to 350F (175C). Butter several baking sheets. Roll dough out on a floured surface to 1/8 inch thick. Using a 2-inch heart-shaped cutter, cut out heart shapes from dough. Using a smaller heart-shaped cutter, cut out hearts from center of 20 of the hearts. Reknead and reroll trimmings and cut out more shapes to make 40 in total, half with centers cut out.

Bake 15 minutes, until very lightly browned. Remove from baking sheets to wire racks to cool. Dust cookies with cut-out centers with powdered sugar. Spread whole hearts with raspberry jam, then top with cut-out cookies.

Makes 20.

JUMBLES

2/3 cup butter, softened
1/2 cup plus 2 tablespoons sugar
1 egg, beaten
2 cups all-purpose flour
1/2 cup ground blanched almonds
Shredded zest of 1 lemon
GLAZE:
2 tablespoons honey
2 tablespoons brown sugar

In a bowl, beat butter with sugar until creamy. Gradually beat in egg.

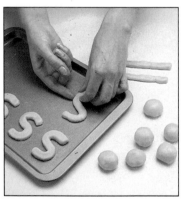

Sift flour onto creamed mixture. Add ground almonds and lemon zest. Mix well to make a firm dough. Knead lightly, then wrap in plastic wrap and refrigerate 30 minutes. Meanwhile, preheat oven to 350F (175C). Grease several baking sheets. Divide dough into 32 equal pieces. Roll each piece into a pencil-thin strip 4 inches long. Twist into an S-shape and place on a baking sheet. Bake 15 minutes, until very lightly browned.

To glaze, in small saucepan, warm honey. Brush warm jumbles with honey, then sprinkle with brown sugar. Return to oven 2 minutes. Cool on baking sheets a few minutes, then remove to wire racks to cool completely.

Makes 32.

GINGER-TOPPED BARS

2 cups all-purpose flour
1 teaspoon ground ginger
1/3 cup sugar
3/4 cup butter, chilled
TOPPING:
1 tablespoon dark corn syrup
1/4 cup butter
2 tablespoons powdered sugar, sifted
1 teaspoon ground ginger

Preheat oven to 350F (175C). Butter an 11″ × 7″ baking pan. Into a bowl, sift flour and ginger, then stir in sugar.

Cut in butter until mixture begins to stick together. Press mixture into prepared pan and smooth top with a spatula. Bake 40 minutes, until very lightly browned.

To make topping, into a small pan, put syrup and butter and heat gently until melted. Stir in powdered sugar and ginger. Pour topping over base while both are still hot. Cool slightly in pan, then cut into rectangles. Remove to wire racks to cool completely.

Makes 16.

— SPICED APRICOT SQUARES —

2 cups all-purpose flour
1 teaspoon apple pie spice
1 cup ground blanched almonds
1 egg, beaten
1-1/2 cups sugar
3/4 cup butter, softened
1/3 cup apricot jam
TO FINISH:
Powdered sugar for sifting

Into a bowl, sift flour and spice. Add ground almonds, egg, sugar and butter. Mix well until thoroughly combined. Knead lightly. Wrap in plastic wrap and refrigerate at least 30 minutes.

Butter an 11″ × 7″ baking pan. Into pan, press half of the dough. Spread apricot jam over dough. On a floured surface, lightly knead remaining dough. Roll out and cut into thin strips. Arrange strips over jam to form a close lattice pattern. Refrigerate 30 minutes. Preheat oven to 350F (175C).

Bake 30 to 40 minutes, until lightly browned. Cool cookies in pan, then sift powdered sugar over top. Cut into 24 squares or bars.

Makes 24.

—— COFFEE-WALNUT COOKIES ——

2 cups all-purpose flour, sifted
1 cup butter, softened
1 cup powdered sugar, sifted
1 egg yolk
1 teaspoon vanilla extract
1-1/4 cups coarsely chopped walnuts
2 tablespoons medium-ground coffee beans
1-1/4 cups walnut pieces

Preheat oven to 350F (175C). Butter several baking sheets.

Into a bowl, sift flour. Add butter, powdered sugar, egg yolk and vanilla. Mix well, then mix in the chopped walnuts and coffee with your hands.

Place heaped teaspoonfuls of mixture on prepared baking sheets. Flatten slightly and top each mound with a walnut piece. Bake 12 to 15 minutes, until just starting to color. Cool on baking sheets a few minutes, then transfer to wire racks to cool completely.

Makes 28 to 30.

LEMON SHORTBREAD

1/2 cup butter, softened
1/4 cup sugar
1-3/4 cups all-purpose flour
1/4 teaspoon grated nutmeg
2 tablespoons cornstarch
Shredded zest of 1 lemon
TO FINISH:
Sugar and grated nutmeg for sprinkling

In a bowl, beat butter with sugar until creamy. Into another bowl, sift flour and nutmeg, then add cornstarch and lemon zest. Blend in creamed butter and sugar with a spoon, then work with your hands to form a soft dough.

On a lightly floured surface, knead until smooth. Roll out to a smooth circle, about 6 inches in diameter. Very lightly flour a 7-inch shortbread mold. Place shortbread, smooth side down, in mold. Press out to fit mold exactly. Very carefully unmold shortbread onto a baking sheet. Refrigerate 1 hour. (If you do not have a shortbread mold, shape dough into a neat circle. Place on baking sheet, prick well with a fork, then pinch edge to decorate.)

Preheat oven to 325F (165C). Bake shortbread 35 to 40 minutes, until cooked through, but still pale in color. As soon as shortbread is removed from oven, sprinkle lightly with sugar and nutmeg. Cool on baking sheet about 20 minutes, then very carefully transfer to a wire rack to cool completely.

Makes 1.

FLORENTINES

1/4 cup unsalted butter
1/3 cup whipping cream
1/3 cup sugar
Finely shredded zest of 1 lemon
1 teaspoon lemon juice
1/2 cup all-purpose flour, sifted
1/2 cup slivered blanched almonds
3/4 cup chopped mixed candied citrus peel
1/3 cup chopped candied cherries
2 tablespoons golden raisins
2 tablespoons chopped angelica
TO FINISH:
3 ounces semisweet chocolate, chopped
3 ounces white chocolate, chopped

Preheat oven to 350F (175C). Grease several baking sheets. Line with parchment paper. Into a saucepan, put butter, cream, sugar, lemon zest and juice. Stir over medium heat until butter melts. Remove from heat and stir in flour, almonds, mixed peel, cherries, golden raisins and angelica. Drop teaspoonfuls of mixture onto baking sheets, spacing well apart. Using a fork dipped in cold water, flatten each mound to a circle about 2-1/2 inches in diameter.

Bake 10 to 12 minutes, until lightly browned around edges. Cool on baking sheets a few minutes, then remove with a spatula to wire racks to cool completely. Melt semisweet and white chocolate separately in 2 heatproof bowls placed over pans of simmering water. Spread flat sides of half the florentines with semisweet chocolate and the remaining florentines with white chocolate. Using a fork, mark chocolate into wavy lines. Leave to set, chocolate sides up.

Makes 28.

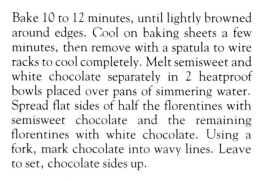

DOUBLE CHOCOLATE COOKIES

1/2 cup butter
1/4 cup granulated sugar
1/3 cup packed brown sugar
1 egg, beaten
1/2 teaspoon vanilla extract
1 cup plus 2 tablespoons all-purpose flour
2 tablespoons unsweetened cocoa powder
1/2 teaspoon baking soda
5 ounces white chocolate pieces, cut into pieces

Preheat oven to 350F (175C). Butter several baking sheets.

In a bowl, beat butter with sugars until creamy. Gradually beat in egg and vanilla extract. Into another bowl, sift flour, cocoa powder and baking soda. Mix well, then stir in chocolate pieces.

Drop teaspoonfuls of dough, well spaced out, onto prepared baking sheets. Bake 10 to 12 minutes, until firm. Cool on baking sheets a few minutes, then remove to wire racks to cool completely.

Makes about 48.

— ORANGE-GLAZED SHORTIES —

1 cup butter, softened
1/3 cup powdered sugar, sifted
Shredded zest of 1 orange
1/2 teaspoon ground coriander
2 cups all-purpose flour
GLAZE:
2 teaspoons apricot jam, heated and strained
3 tablespoons powdered sugar, sifted
1 tablespoon orange juice

Butter several baking sheets and dust lightly with flour.

In a bowl, beat butter with powdered sugar until very light and creamy. Stir in the orange zest. Into another bowl, sift the coriander and flour, then work into creamy mixture with a wooden spoon to form a soft dough. Put dough into a pastry bag fitted with a large star tip. Pipe rings of dough onto prepared baking sheets. Refrigerate 30 minutes. Preheat oven to 350F (175C). Bake cookies 20 minutes, until very lightly browned.

To glaze, brush each shortie with a little apricot jam. In a small bowl, mix together the powdered sugar and orange juice and brush over cookies. Return cookies to oven 2 to 3 minutes, until glaze is set. Cool on baking sheets a few minutes, then transfer to wire racks to cool completely.

Makes 25 to 28.

—CHERRY-NUT SHORTBREAD—

SHORTCAKE:
1-1/2 cups all-purpose flour
1/4 cup sugar
1/2 cup butter, chilled
TOPPING:
1/2 cup coarsely chopped Brazil nuts
1/2 cup quartered candied cherries
3 tablespoons honey

Preheat oven to 325F (165C). Grease a 7-inch loose-bottomed tart pan.

Into a bowl, sift flour, Add sugar and cut in butter until dough begins to stick together. Press dough into prepared pan. Smooth top with a spatula. Bake 35 minutes, until very lightly browned. Cool completely in pan.

To make topping, into a small saucepan, put nuts, cherries and honey. Bring to a boil, then simmer 2 minutes, until sticky. Spread mixture evenly over cooled shortcake. Cool. When topping is set, cut shortbread into 8 wedges.

Makes 8.

CHOCOLATE CHECKERBOARDS

3/4 cup butter, softened
3/4 cup sugar
1 teaspoon vanilla extract
2 eggs
4-1/2 cups all-purpose flour
2 teaspoons baking powder
1 teaspoon milk
2 tablespoons unsweetened cocoa powder

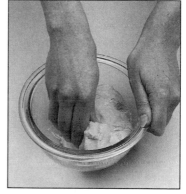

Grease several baking sheets. Divide butter and sugar equally between 2 bowls.

To make vanilla dough, in a bowl, beat half of the butter and sugar until light and fluffy. Beat in vanilla and 1 egg. In another bowl, sift half of the flour and 1 teaspoon baking powder. Blend in with spoon, then work by hand to form a smooth dough. Make chocolate dough in same way with remaining butter, sugar and egg, adding milk and sifting in cocoa powder with remaining flour and baking powder. Divide each portion of dough into 4 equal pieces.

On a floured surface, roll each piece of dough into a rope 12 inches long. Place 1 chocolate rope next to a vanilla one. Place a chocolate one on top of the vanilla one and a vanilla one on top of the chocolate. Press firmly together to form a square. Wrap in plastic wrap. Repeat with remaining dough. Refrigerate 1 hour. Preheat oven to 350F (175C). Cut dough into 48 slices and place on baking sheets. Bake 20 minutes, until lightly browned. Cool on wire racks.

Makes 48.

LEMON CURD

4 lemons
1-3/4 cups sugar
1-1/2 cups butter
4 eggs, beaten

Into a heatproof bowl, finely grate zest of lemons. Squeeze lemons and pour juice into bowl. Stir in sugar. Cut butter into small pieces and add to other ingredients.

Set bowl over a saucepan one-quarter filled with simmering water and stir until butter has melted and sugar dissolved. Strain eggs into lemon mixture.

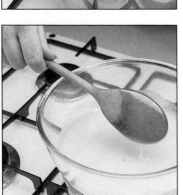

Cook gently, stirring frequently, 10 to 15 minutes, until mixture is thick and creamy. Pour into clean, warm jars and seal while hot. Keep in the refrigerator.

Makes about 1-1/2 pounds.

Variations: For Lime Curd, use limes instead of lemons.

For Lemon & Elderflower Curd, add 2 handfuls of elderberry flowers, well shaken and flowers removed from stems, after adding butter.

APPLE BUTTER

5 cups dry cider
2-1/2 pounds Golden Delicious apples
1 pound Granny Smith apples
Sugar
Grated zest and juice of 1/2 orange
Grated zest and juice of 1/2 lemon
1/2 teaspoon ground cinnamon
1/2 teaspoon ground cloves

Into a large saucepan, put cider. Boil rapidly until reduced by one-third. With a knife, peel, core and slice apples, then add to pan.

If necessary, add enough water to just cover apples. Half cover pan and simmer until apples are very soft and pulpy and well reduced. Stir occasionally and crush pulp down in pan as it cooks. Measure pulp and process to a puree if it is lumpy. Return to saucepan. Add 1-1/2 cups sugar for every 2-1/2 cups of apple pulp. Stir in orange and lemon zests and juices, cinnamon and cloves.

Cook gently until sugar has dissolved. Simmer, stirring frequently, until most moisture has been driven off. The mixture is ready when a spoon drawn across the surface leaves an impression. Spoon into clean, warm jars and store in the refrigerator. Once a jar is opened, apple butter should be consumed within 3 to 4 days.

Makes 4 or 5 small jars.

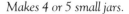

—CUMBERLAND RUM BUTTER—

1/2 cup butter, softened
1-1/2 cups packed dark brown sugar
1/4 teaspoon ground cinnamon
2 tablespoons dark rum
TO SERVE:
Hot toast, muffins or crumpets
TO DECORATE:
Orange zest

Into a bowl, put butter and beat until soft. Gradually beat in sugar.

Gradually beat in the cinnamon and rum. Pile mixture into a small dish. Cover and refrigerate until firm. Decorate with orange zest. Serve with hot toast, muffins or crumpets.

Makes 6 to 8 servings.

Variation: For Anchovy Butter, instead of sugar, cinnamon and rum, work 1-1/2 ounces drained, canned anchovies into butter. Serve on toast.

ROSE PETAL JAM

1/2 pound fragrant, red rose petals
2 cups sugar
4-1/2 cups water
Juice of 2 lemons

Cut off white area from bottom of each petal. Into a bowl, put petals and sprinkle with enough of the sugar to cover them. Leave overnight.

In a saucepan, put remaining sugar, the water and lemon juice. Heat gently until sugar has dissolved. Stir in rose petals and simmer 20 minutes. Bring to a boil and boil 5 minutes, until mixture thickens.

Pour jam into clean, warm jars. Cover and label. Store in a cool place.

Makes about 1 pound.

ICED ROSE TEA

3 tablespoons Ceylon breakfast tea, or to taste
4-1/4 cups lukewarm water
Sugar, to taste
Few drops rosewater, to taste
12 ice cubes
6 mint sprigs
Fresh rose petals

Into a bowl, put tea. Pour warm water over tea and let stand overnight.

Strain tea into a large pitcher. Stir in sugar and rosewater, then add ice cubes. Place a mint sprig and a few rose petals in each of 6 glasses. Pour tea on top.

Makes 6 servings.

Variations: For Vanilla Iced Tea, omit rosewater. Instead, put a vanilla bean in the bowl with tea to soak overnight. Remove it before serving.

For Mint Tea, omit the rosewater and rose petals. Put a mint sprig in bowl with tea to soak overnight. Remove it before serving. Place a fresh mint sprig in each glass.

SPICED TEA

Small piece gingerroot, peeled
4 whole cloves
1-inch stick cinnamon
2 tablespoons Ceylon tea
1/4 cup sugar
1/3 cup orange juice
Juice of 1/2 lemon
TO DECORATE:
4 to 6 cinnamon sticks

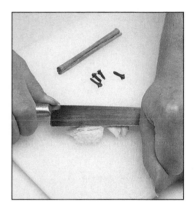

Bruise ginger. In a saucepan, combine ginger-root, cloves, cinnamon and 4-1/2 cups cold water. Bring to a boil.

Into a heatproof bowl, put tea. Pour boiling spiced water over tea, then steep 5 minutes. Add sugar and stir until dissolved, then stir in orange and lemon juices.

Reheat before serving, but do not simmer or boil. Strain spiced tea into heatproof glasses. Serve with a cinnamon stick in each glass.

Makes 4 to 6 servings.

Note: This drink is also delicious served chilled.

Variation: To make Party Punch, add extra sugar, to taste, then just before serving, add 1-1/4 cups rum.

TENNIS CUP

1 cup sugar
2/3 cup water
1 lemon
2 oranges
2 (750-ml.) bottles red or white wine
2-1/2 cups soda water
TO DECORATE:
Thin cucumber and orange slices
Borage flowers or violets, if available

Into a saucepan, put sugar and water. Cook over low heat, stirring, until sugar has dissolved. Bring to a boil, then boil until syrup reaches 220F (105C) on a candy thermometer.

With a vegetable peeler, thinly pare peel from lemon and oranges. Add to syrup and simmer gently 10 minutes. Set aside until completely cold.

Squeeze juice from lemon and oranges and strain into syrup, then pour in the wine and refrigerate until chilled. Just before serving, add soda water. Pour into glasses. Decorate with cucumber and orange slices and borage sprigs or violets.

Makes about 9 cups.

SUMMER TEA CUP

1 Lapsang Souchong tea bag
2-1/2 cups boiling water
4 teaspoons brown sugar
1-1/4 cups pineapple juice
1/3 cup white rum
2-1/2 cups ginger ale
Ice cubes
TO DECORATE:
Pieces fresh pineapple

In a heatproof bowl, place tea bag and boiling water.

Leave tea to steep 5 minutes, then remove tea bag. Stir in brown sugar and leave until cold. Stir pineapple juice and rum into tea.

Just before serving, pour ginger ale into tea. Add ice cubes. Place a few pieces of pineapple in each glass and pour in the chilled tea.

Makes about 6-3/4 cups.

—OLD-FASHIONED LEMONADE—

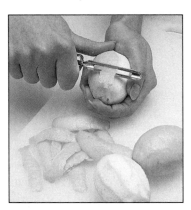

3 lemons
1/2 cup sugar
TO FINISH:
Ice
Mint sprigs
Lemon slices

Using a vegetable peeler, thinly pare peel from lemons and put in a heatproof bowl or large pitcher with sugar. Squeeze juice from lemons into a bowl and set aside.

Bring 3-1/4 cups water to a boil and pour over lemon peel and sugar. Stir to dissolve sugar, then let cool completely. Add lemon juice and strain into a pitcher. Refrigerate until chilled. Serve in ice-filled tumblers, decorated with mint and lemon slices.

Makes 6 servings.

Variations: To make Pink Lemonade, add just enough pink grenadine syrup to each glass to give lemonade a pale pink color. Omit mint and lemon slices and decorate each glass with a cherry.

To make Orangeade, use 3 oranges and 1 lemon instead of 3 lemons. Omit mint and lemon slices and decorate with orange slices.

—GRAPEFRUIT BARLEY WATER—

1/3 cup pearl barley
1/4 cup sugar
2 pink grapefruit
TO DECORATE:
Mint leaves

Into a saucepan, put barley. Just cover with cold water and bring to a boil. Pour barley into a strainer and rinse under cold water.

Return barley to saucepan. Add 2-1/2 cups cold water and bring to a boil again. Cover and simmer 1 hour. Strain liquid into a pitcher, stir in the sugar and leave until completely cold.

Squeeze juice from grapefruit and add to cooled barley water. Refrigerate until chilled. Serve decorated with mint leaves.

Makes about 2-1/2 cups.

Variation: To make Lemon Barley Water, use 2 lemons instead of grapefruit.

Clockwise from top:

SALMON PINWHEELS
page 19

TURKEY TRIANGLES
page 17

AVOCADO & BACON SANDWICHES
page 15

SPICY CHICKEN SANDWICHES
page 16

Clockwise from top right:

SMOKED SALMON CROÛTES
page 27

SALAMI PUFFS
page 22

MINI QUICHES
page 30

CHEESE STRAWS
page 32

CRAB & GINGER TRIANGLES
page 25

DEVILED HAM TOASTS
page 23

PARMESAN BEIGNETS
page 28

Center:

SCOTCH EGGS
page 33

Clockwise from top left:

CRANBERRY-BRAZIL LOAF
page 43

BLACKBERRY MUFFINS
page 37

CRUMPETS
page 48

CHEESE & CHIVE BRAID
page 45

WELSH CAKES
page 38

APPLE BISCUIT ROUND
page 36

CARAWAY KUGELHOPF
page 42

Center:

LEMON & CURRANT BRIOCHES
page 47

CHELSEA BUNS
page 46

Clockwise from top right:

LEMON CRUNCH CAKE
page 50

COCONUT & CHERRY CAKE
page 53

DUNDEE CAKE
page 54

GINGER CAKE
page 51

APPLE STREUSEL CAKE
page 55

TOFFEE DATE CAKE
page 58

PEACH & ORANGE CAKE
page 59

Center:

CHOCOLATE MARBLE CAKE
page 57

Clockwise from top:

BLACK CURRANT WHIRLS
page 60

QUEEN CAKES
page 68

STRAWBERRY-ROSE MERINGUES
page 61

LEMON BUTTERFLY CUPCAKES
page 69

HONEY MADELEINES
page 62

CHOCOLATE BROWNIES
page 63

SPONGE DROPS
page 66

GINGER BRANDY SNAPS
page 67

Clockwise from top right:

FROSTED WALNUT CAKE
page 75

SUMMER CAKE
page 70

DOUBLE CHOCOLATE GÂTEAU
page 72

PINEAPPLE-CARROT CAKE
page 76

LEMON MOUSSE GÂTEAU
page 78

COFFEE-CARAMEL CAKE
page 80

Center:

CHOCOLATE ORANGE CAKE
page 77

Clockwise from top:

PALMIERS
page 83

SUMMER FRUIT TARTLETS
page 85

MAPLE-PECAN TARTLETS
page 86

NUTTY FILO FINGERS
page 88

FRANGIPANE TARTLETS
page 89

MAIDS OF HONOR
page 82

Clockwise from top:

JUMBLES
page 92

ORANGE-GLAZED SHORTIES
page 99

SPICED APRICOT SQUARES
page 94

LINZER HEARTS
page 91

COFFEE-WALNUT COOKIES
page 95

CHERRY-NUT SHORTBREAD
page 100

ALMOND MACAROONS
page 90

INDEX

Almond Macaroons, 90, 119
Apple Biscuit Round, 36, 114
Apple Butter, 103
Apple Streusel Cake, 55, 115
Avocado & Bacon
  Sandwiches, 15, 112

Black Currant Whirls, 60,
  116
Blackberry Muffins, 37, 114

Caraway Kugelhopf, 42, 114
Cheese & Chive Braid, 45,
  114
Cheese Straws, 32, 113
Chelsea Buns, 46, 114
Cherry-Nut Bread, 9, 41
Cherry-Nut Rocks, 65
Cherry-Nut Shortbread, 100,
  119
Choc-Almond Meringue, 74
Chocolate Brownies, 63, 116
Chocolate Checkerboards, 9,
  101
Chocolate Marble Cake, 57,
  115
Chocolate-Nut Muffins, 39
Chocolate-Orange Cake, 77,
  117
Coconut & Cherry Cake, 53,
  115
Coffee-Caramel Cake, 80,
  117
Coffee-Walnut Cookies, 95,
  119
Crab & Ginger Triangles, 25,
  113
Cranberry-Brazil Loaf, 43,
  114
Crumpets, 48, 114
Cucumber & Dill Hearts, 8,
  10
Cumberland Rum Butter, 104

Date & Walnut Loaf, 40
Date & Walnut Sandwiches,
  21
Deviled Ham Toasts, 23, 113
Devonshire Splits, 49

Double Chocolate Cookies,
  98
Double Chocolate Gâteau,
  72, 117
Dundee Cake, 54, 115

Egg & Sprout Circles, 8, 11

Florentines, 97
Frangipane Tartlets, 89, 118
Frosted Walnut Cake, 75, 117

Ginger Brandy Snaps, 67, 116
Ginger Cake, 51, 115
Ginger-Topped Bars, 93
Grapefruit Barley Water, 111

Honey Madeleines, 62, 116
Honey Spice Cake, 56

Iced Rose Tea, 106
Italian Tempters, 12

Jewel-Topped Madeira Cake,
  9, 52
Jumbles, 92, 119

Leek & Bacon Knots, 44
Lemon & Currant Brioches,
  8, 47, 114
Lemon Butterfly Cupcakes,
  69, 116
Lemon Crunch Cake, 50, 115
Lemon Curd, 9, 102
Lemon Custard Slices, 87
Lemon Mousse Gâteau, 8, 78,
  117
Lemon Shortbread, 96
Linzer Hearts, 91, 119

Maids of Honor, 82, 118
Maple-Pecan Tarts, 86, 118
Mini Quiches, 30, 113

Nutty Filo Fingers, 88, 118

Old-Fashioned Lemonade,
  110
Orange-Glazed Shorties, 9,
  99, 119

Palmiers, 83, 118
Parmesan Beignets, 28, 113
Pastrami Sandwiches, 14
Peach & Orange Cake, 59,
  115
Pineapple-Carrot Cake, 76,
  117
Potted Shrimp, 24
Potted Stilton, 31

Queen Cakes, 68, 116

Raspberry Eclairs, 84
Rose Petal Jam, 105

Salami Puffs, 22, 113
Salmon Pinwheels, 19, 112
Scones, 34
Scotch Eggs, 33
Scotch Pancakes, 35
Shrimp Fingers, 18
Smoked Salmon Croûtes, 27,
  113
Spiced Apricot Squares, 94,
  119
Spiced Tea, 107
Spicy Chicken Sandwiches,
  16, 112
Sponge Drops, 66, 116
Stilton & Pear Pockets, 20
Strawberry Roulade, 71
Strawberry Shortcake, 64
Strawberry-Rose Meringues,
  61, 116
Striped Sandwiches, 8, 13
Summer Cake, 70, 117
Summer Fruit Tartlets, 85,
  118
Summer Tea Cup, 109

Tennis Cup, 108
Tia Maria Choux Ring, 81
Toffee Date Cake, 58, 115
Tuna Toasties, 26
Turkey Triangles, 17,
  112

Welsh Cakes, 38, 114
Welsh Rabbit Fingers, 29